Biographical Sk
for
Listening and Reading

# NOBEL PRIZE WINNERS

## BY LISA F. DEWITT

# PRO LINGUA ASSOCIATES

Published by Pro Lingua Associates
15 Elm Street
Brattleboro, Vermont 05301

SAN 216-0579

802-257-7779

*At Pro Lingua,*
*our objective is to foster*
*an approach to learning and teaching which*
*we call **Interplay**, the interaction of language*
*learners and teachers with their materials,*
*with the language and the culture, and*
*with each other in active, creative,*
*and productive **play**.*

ISBN 0-86647-047-6

The publisher wishes to thank The Nobel Foundation in Stockholm, Sweden,
for their permission to reproduce the official photographic portraits of the
Nobel prize winners used in this book.

The publisher also wishes to thank Michael Jerald for obtaining the portraits
following a suggestion by Barbara George.

This book was set in Bodoni by Stevens Graphics of Brattleboro, Vermont, and
printed and bound by Capital City Press of Montpelier, Vermont.

Designed by Arthur A. Burrows.

Printed in the United States of America.

# Dedication

To the 1985-1987 students of the Adiestramiento En Inglés program, C.I.D.L.E., at the University of Guadalajara, México, whose spirit, humor, insight, and intelligence continue to inspire me.

# Acknowledgements

Thanks to Andy Burrows who liked my ideas, saw the possibilities, and encouraged me.

Special thanks to Ray Clark who was my editor and responsible for the development of the listening exercises. His subtle editing and input were invaluable.

# Contents

# Introduction

## *To the Student:*

This is a collection of biographies on Nobel Prize winners. They are divided into the six Nobel Prize categories: Peace, Literature, Economics, Physiology or Medicine, Physics, and Chemistry. Some of the countries that these people represent are: South Africa, India, Tibet, the United States, Poland, the Soviet Union, Germany, Egypt, England, China, Colombia, Sweden, and France.

The selections are arranged from easy to difficult. Many of the key words are repeated in the selections and the number of blanks in the exercises increase as the selections become more difficult.

There are two tapes. On one tape, the readings are slow and deliberate. On the other, the readings are faster. Use either tape or use the slow one the first time you listen, and use the fast one for review.

If you are using the workbook and tapes for self-study, you can follow this simple procedure.

1.  Take a moment to look at the person's picture, name, and brief biographical statement. Think about what you already know about the person. Ask yourself what you would like to learn about him or her.

2.  Read the passage. Circle the words that you don't know or cannot figure out from the context (the surrounding words).

3.  Look at the key words and add any words you circled that are not already on the list.

4.  *Optional:* Play the tape and read along using the completed text. See if you can now recognize some of the key words that you weren't sure of.

5.  Look up in a dictionary those words that you don't know or can't figure out.

6.  Turn to the listening exercise and play the tape. If you are unsure of a word or don't have time to write the entire word, then try to write the first letter of the word in the blank.

7.  Rewind the tape and play it again. Fill in all the blanks.

8. *Optional:* Play the tape again and read along — out loud.

9. Ask yourself:

   What did I learn about the person?
   Did I learn what I wanted to know about him or her?
   What new words did I learn?
   What more would I like to know about him or her?

10. *Optional:* See what else you can learn about the person using:

    Encyclopedias
    Biographical Journals
    Magazine and Newspaper Articles
    Books written by or about the person

11. *Optional:* Look at the complete list of Nobel Prize winners from 1901 to the present and do your own research, reading and writing on another person of interest to you.

## *To the Teacher:*

This collection of biographical sketches on Nobel Prize winners is written for the intermediate ESL level and for any middle school, high school, and adult education students working on basic listening, reading, and vocabulary skills. The selections increase in difficulty from beginning to end as do the exercises. Some of the key words are repeated throughout the collection so that the blanks in the listening exercises are cumulative.

There are two tapes. One is slow and deliberate; the other is fast. Use the one that is appropriate for your class or use them both; the slow one for the initial listening phase and the fast one for review.

A few possibilities of how you may choose to use the workbook and the tapes are as:

an on-going language laboratory activity;

a short, on-going, in-class listening/reading activity for 10–20 minutes each day;

a discussion starter;

an independent study for individual students;

a reading-writing-listening-speaking expansion activity. Students do the research on a Nobel Prize winner of their choosing and make individual or group presentations to the class.

Use the basic procedure suggested for student self-study. You can direct the steps and decide when to use the fast or slow tape and what optional steps to use.

It is not recommended that the key words be pretaught or presented before the students have a chance to read the selection. The reasons are: to allow the students to figure out new words using context, and to encourage reading and listening for meaning rather than for isolated words. Step #4 of the procedure is optional and was included because it is possible that there would be words that are unfamiliar to the student in the written form but understood when they are heard.

## PREPARING TO READ AND LISTEN

When the teacher involves the students in an initial preparation phase, students are more motivated to read and to listen and comprehension is enhanced. This phase includes: drawing upon the students' prior knowledge or experience with the subject; using pictures, slides, poems, quotes, songs, videos, etc. to expand the students' knowledge; and allowing time for students to generate predictions and expectations about the content of the selection.

## *ENJOY!*

# Alfred Bernhard Nobel

(1833 — 1896)

Swedish chemist and inventor

*The founder of the Nobel Prize Foundation.*

# Alfred Bernhard Nobel

Alfred Nobel was born on October 21, 1833 in Stockholm, Sweden. He was the third son of Swedish inventor Immanuel Nobel. All three sons worked in their father's business of manufacturing explosives. Alfred invented dynamite, an explosive which is used in the construction of roads, railroads, and canals. He became very wealthy from the sales of his explosives.

Nobel thought that his scientific work was his major contribution to world progress, but because of his interest in peace, science, and literature he established a fund. He stated that the interest from the fund would be given as prizes to those who provided great benefits for mankind. His fund has made the name Nobel well-known throughout the world.

Alfred Nobel died on December 10, 1896. A few years after his death the Nobel Foundation of Stockholm was established. The first prizes were awarded in 1901 in the fields of physics, chemistry, physiology or medicine, literature, and peace. In 1969 a prize in the field of economics was established by the Central Bank of Sweden.

The winners in physics, chemistry, and economics are named by the Royal Swedish Academy of Sciences. The physiology or medicine prize is awarded by the Caroline Institute in Stockholm. The peace prize is awarded by a committee of five people elected by the Norwegian Parliament.

The amount of each award has increased from about $30,000 to over $400,000. Prizes are awarded each year. If in a certain year a prize is not awarded in a field, the money is held in the Nobel Prize fund. Prizes, however, must be awarded every five years. A single prize may be divided among two or three winners, and it is possible to win twice. The peace prize has been awarded to individuals and to organizations such as the International Red Cross and Amnesty International.

It is interesting that the name Nobel is associated with dynamite and peace. Alfred Nobel knew the destructive power of explosives, but he was a pacifist at heart. As he once said, "Perhaps if a very terrible weapon of war could be invented, then it would be necessary for nations to turn to peace."

*See page 53 for Listening Exercise 1.*

2

# Desmond Tutu

(1931 —       )

Black African Anglican Bishop

*Awarded the Nobel Peace Prize in 1984 for his work in advocating nonviolent resistance to apartheid.*

# Desmond Tutu

Bishop Desmond Mpilo Tutu was born on October 7, 1931 in Klerks-dorp in the Western Transvaal, which is part of South Africa. Tutu graduated from the University of South Africa in 1954. He was a school teacher from 1955 until 1958, when he entered St. Peter's Theological College in Rosettenville, Johannesburg. In 1960 he graduated and became a deacon. Between 1962 and 1966 Tutu, with his wife and children, lived in London, England, where he received his master's degree in theology.

Years later, in 1975, Tutu became the first black Dean of the Anglican Church. Then in 1985, he became Johannesburg's first black Anglican Bishop.

Bishop Tutu voices the problems and goals of many black South Africans. He is not a politician, and yet he is involved in political issues. He says of his involvement, "I cannot help it when I see injustice. I cannot keep quiet."

He wants equal citizenship for South African blacks, the abolition of the apartheid system, and a common educational system that will change the quality of South African society.

His message includes nonviolent solutions. He advocates the ideals and principles that Martin Luther King, Jr., died for. Tutu has taken a firm stand against the evils of apartheid and is recognized internationally for his courage and peaceful efforts to establish a democratic and just society in South Africa. In 1984 he was awarded the Nobel Peace Prize.

Bishop Tutu describes apartheid as being "as evil and as vicious as Nazism and Communism."

He also speaks of the vision of the unification of the black and white communities. He believes that South Africa can teach the world "what unity in diversity really is about."

*See page 57 for Listening Exercise 2*

God bless you
M. Teresa mc

# Mother Teresa of Calcutta

(1911 —        )

Nun and founder of a
Roman Catholic order—the Missionaries of Charity

*Awarded the Nobel Peace Prize in 1979 for her
compassionate service to the poorest of the poor.*

# Mother Teresa of Calcutta

Mother Teresa is internationally respected for her work in relieving the sufferings of the poor, the abandoned, and the dying.

She was born on August 27, 1910, in Skopje, Yugoslavia. She attended a local government school, and as a young student there, she became a member of a Catholic association for children. She was only twelve years old when she knew that she wanted to dedicate her life to helping others. At the age of eighteen, she entered the order of the Sisters of Our Lady of Loreto. She taught in the order's schools in Calcutta, India, until September 10, 1946, when she had "the call within a call." This call was her heart telling her that she should help the poor while living among them.

In February 1948, Mother Teresa was granted special permission from the Vatican to leave the convent "in order to spend herself in the service of the poor and the needy in the slums of Calcutta, and to gather around her some companions ready to undertake the same work." On August 16, 1948, she took off the religious clothes of the Loreto nun and put on a cheap, simple, white sari with a blue border, a small cross pinned to the left shoulder, and open sandals on her feet. She began her new service by bringing dying people from the streets into a home where they could die in peace and with dignity.

Mother Teresa has since established many homes for the dying, orphanages for the hundreds of sick, unwanted, or abandoned children, schools for these children, and leper clinics. She says, "Any work of love brings a person face to face with God."

In 1959, she founded a Roman Catholic order—the Missionaries of Charity. These sisters, brothers, and co-workers have committed themselves to serve the poorest of the poor all over the world. Mother Teresa served as the head of the order until 1990 when she resigned due to poor health.

Mother Teresa's compassionate service was recognized internationally when she was awarded the Nobel Peace Prize in 1979. Her message to mankind may be simply stated in her own words: "We can do no great things—only small things with great love."

*See page 61 for Listening Exercise 3*

# Elie Wiesel

(1928 —          )

Romanian Jewish novelist, journalist, lecturer, and
university professor

*Awarded the Nobel Peace Prize in 1986. The Nobel
Committee said that he is an important spiritual leader
and guide.*

7

# Elie Wiesel

Elie Wiesel is a Jewish novelist, journalist, lecturer, and spokesman for the survivors of the Holocaust—the Nazi effort to destroy the Jewish people during World War II.

He was born on September 30, 1928, in Sighet, Romania. Elie was only sixteen when he and his mother, father, and three sisters were sent to the Nazi concentration camp in Auschwitz, Poland.

During the Nazi regime, Jews throughout Europe were sent to concentration camps. These camps were death camps. The living conditions were inhumane. People died of illness and starvation, and others were killed in the gas chambers. Approximately six million Jews died during the Holocaust. When the war ended in 1945, Elie, his two older sisters, and all the other camp survivors were freed.

Elie Wiesel has devoted his life to being a witness and spokesman. He says that, as a Jew, one must do this. As a Jew, one must be a link between the dead of the Holocaust and today's world. As a Jew, one must be a link between the Jew and the non-Jew. In his writing and teaching he retells the story of that tragic time in the world's history so that history will not repeat itself. His message is that only by remembering can we hope to prevent future holocausts: "Memory may perhaps be our only answer. Our only hope to save the world from ultimate punishment, a nuclear holocaust."

Today, he lives in New York City with his wife Marion, her daughter Jennifer, and their son Elisha. He commutes one day a week to Boston, Massachusetts, where he is a professor of religion at Boston University. He has written over thirty books, and in 1983 he won the International Literary Prize for Peace. In 1986 he was the recipient of the Nobel Peace Prize. The Nobel Committee said that Elie Wiesel is "one of the most important spiritual leaders and guides," and that his message is "one of peace, atonement, and dignity."

At the World Gathering of Jewish Holocaust Survivors in Jerusalem in June 1981, Elie Wiesel, with 7,000 others, pledged that the Holocaust "must never be forgotten, never be repeated." Never Again.

*See page 65 for Listening Exercise 4.*

# The Dalai Lama

(1935 —        )

Tibetan Buddhist monk, monarch, and religious leader

*Awarded the Nobel Peace Prize in 1989 for advocating
"peaceful solutions based upon tolerance and mutual
respect in order to preserve the historical and cultural
heritage of his people."*

# The Dalai Lama

The Fourteenth Dalai Lama says of himself, "I am a simple Buddhist monk, no more, no less." But to the people of Tibet, he is their monarch and religious leader. The title, "Dalai Lama" means "Ocean of Wisdom." The followers of Buddha believe he is the reincarnation of the first "Buddha of Mercy," who appeared in 1391 and whose purpose was and continues to be to protect all living beings. When one Dalai Lama dies another is born to continue to help mankind. To the Tibetans, the Dalai Lama represents the Tibetan way of life.

The Fourteenth Dalai Lama was born on June 6, 1935, in the small farming village of Taktser, Tibet. Taktser is about 9,000 feet above the sea, and the people grow wheat and barley. The Dalai Lama was born into a large family and lived as a farmer's son until he was four years old.

The Thirteenth Dalai Lama died in 1933, and the search began for the Fourteenth. The Lamaist monks searched the many towns and villages of Tibet. They came to Taktser, and after passing several tests the two-year-old son of a farmer was recognized as the Fourteenth Dalai Lama. At the age of four-and-a-half, he was formally recognized and he sat on the Lion Throne in the holy city of Lhasa as the ruler of Tibet. The young Dalai Lama was educated in the thousand-room Potala Palace overlooking Lhasa. His family did not live in the Palace with him; they lived in a house near the Palace, and he visited them at least once a month.

In 1950, when the Dalai Lama was fifteen, the Chinese Communist armies of Mao Tse-Tung invaded Tibet. The Communists claimed that Tibet was part of China. The Tibetans, however, claimed that racially, culturally, and geographically they were a separate country. In 1959, the Dalai Lama went into exile in India. The Chinese Communist domination continues today, and the Tibetans continue to suffer. The Dalai Lama says:

> I would dare say that no people have suffered more since the Second World War; and their sufferings have not ended, they are continuing every day, and they will continue until the Chinese leave our country, or until Tibetans have ceased to exist as a race or as a religious community.

The Dalai Lama has tried for over thirty years to keep the world interested in the cause of Tibet's independence, even though he continues to live in exile in India.

In 1989, the Dalai Lama was awarded the Nobel Peace Prize for advocating "peaceful solutions based upon tolerance and mutual respect in order to preserve the historical and cultural heritage of his people."

Honoring the Dalai Lama can be seen as the world's support for Tibetan freedom. The Dalai Lama himself has expressed his hope in this way:

> My hope rests in the courage of the Tibetans, and the love of truth and justice which is still in the heart of the human race; and my faith is in the compassion of Lord Buddha.

*See page 69 for Listening Exercise 5.*

# Martin Luther King, Jr.

(1929 — 1968)

American clergyman and civil rights leader

*Awarded the Nobel Peace Prize in 1964 for his nonviolent struggle against racial oppression.*

# Martin Luther King, Jr.

Dr. Martin Luther King, Jr., was a man of peace who devoted his life to the struggle for equal civil rights for the poor, the disadvantaged, and the racially oppressed in the United States. He is considered to be the most influential civil rights leader of the 1950's and 1960's.

King was born on January 15, 1929, in Atlanta, Georgia. He was the second of three children, and his father was a Baptist minister. He was an excellent student and graduated from college with honors at the age of nineteen. Later, in 1951, he graduated first in his class from theological school, and in 1955 he received his Ph.D. in theology.

As a student in theological school, King studied the life and teachings of Mahatma Gandhi of India. King's own personal and religious philosophies were strongly influenced by Gandhi. King taught, preached, and practiced Gandhi's doctrine of nonviolent civil disobedience.

In 1953, King married Coretta Scott and then in 1954 took a job as a Baptist minister in Montgomery, Alabama. Later, in 1955, Rosa Parks, a black woman and member of his church, was arrested for refusing to give up her seat on the bus to a white man. This incident started the civil rights movement in the United States. King became involved by organizing a bus boycott in Montgomery. This boycott and others contributed to an important new law when in 1956 the Supreme Court ruled that segregation on public transportation was illegal.

In 1957 King helped to found the Southern Christian Leadership Conference whose purpose was to coordinate the many civil rights organizations. In his work for SCLC, King travelled and spoke in many cities all over the United States. While he was in New York City, in 1958, there was an assassination attempt. However, this did not stop King or the growing civil rights movement.

In response to the movement, President John F. Kennedy sent a civil rights bill to Congress. In 1964 Congress finally passed the Civil Rights Act. This act was important because, for the first time, there was a law to protect voting rights, to provide access to public accommodations, to desegregate public facilities and public education, and to provide equal employment opportunities. This same year, Martin Luther King, Jr., became the youngest recipient of the Nobel Peace Prize.

Then, on April 4, 1968, while in Memphis, Tennessee, to support a strike by black workers, King was assassinated. Many thousands of people—black and white—mourned his death. The United States, and indeed the world, had lost a symbol of hope.

King's dream was that one day:

> . . . all of God's children, black men and white men, Jews and Gentiles, Protestants and Catholics, will be able to join hands and sing in the words of the old Negro spiritual, "Free at last! Free at last! Thank God Almighty, we are free at last."

*See page 73 for Listening Exercise 6.*

# Lech Walesa

(1943 —          )

Polish electrician, labor activist and leader of Solidarity

*Awarded the Nobel Peace Prize in 1983 for his
"determination to solve his country's problems
through negotiation and cooperation without
resorting to violence."*

15

# Lech Walesa

In Poland in 1989, for the first time in history, a communist government was peacefully defeated in free elections. This remarkable event was the result of the slow and steady growth of Solidarity, a trade union. Under the leadership of Lech Walesa, Solidarity slowly developed throughout the 70's and 80's into a powerful political force. Poland — Solidarity —Walesa: these three words are inseparable.

Lech Walesa was born on September 29, 1943, in Popow, Poland. His father, Boleslaw Walesa, was a carpenter who died two months after he was released from doing hard labor in one of the Nazi work camps. Lech was only eighteen months old at the time. His mother, Feliksa Walesa, married her husband's brother, Stanislaw Walesa, a year later. There were seven children, and they all worked on the family's small farm. Their home was small and without electricity. And so, this was the humble beginning of a man who inspired his country towards freedom from the oppressive rule of Communism. Lech Walesa has been called "a political genius, an instinctive leader who knows what the crowd is thinking before the crowd knows it, an apostle of nonviolence in the tradition of Gandhi and Martin Luther King."

After Walesa received his training at a vocational school in Lipno, Poland, he started working as an electrician at a shipyard in the Baltic port of Gdansk, Poland. By 1976 he was labeled a troublemaker because of his activities with the workers union at the shipyard. He was fired from his job. His work with the union, however, continued. Then in 1980, the Solidarity movement was formed as the first independent trade union in a Soviet-controlled country. In September 1981, Walesa was elected president of Solidarity and called for many economic and social reforms.

By December 1981, the Communist government imposed martial law, and leaders of the trade unions, opposition groups, intellectuals, and some clergy were arrested. Walesa was taken to a cabin in the wilderness where he stayed for eleven months under the guard of the government. After he was released in November 1982, he was watched and followed closely. The Solidarity movement was outlawed but remained active, and Walesa secretly met with the Temporary Coordinating Committee of Solidarity. Throughout its history, Solidarity has used nonviolent means to achieve its goals, and in 1983 Walesa was awarded the Nobel Peace Prize for his "determination to solve his country's problems through negotiation and cooperation without resorting to violence."

Walesa did not travel to Oslo, Norway, to accept the prize because he feared that he would not be allowed back into Poland. His wife, Daunta, went in his place and delivered his speech. That night, outside their apartment window, a crowd of supporters gathered, and Lech Walesa said:

> I see this as a prize for us all, as a reward to each of us who wished to attain the truth by following the course of nonviolence and common understanding. I believe that if foreigners can understand us . . . then sooner or later we will be recognized by authorities in our own country. I still believe the day will come when we will sit down together at the same table and come to an understanding about what is best for Poland, because whether we like it or not, we have no choice but to come to an understanding; there is no other solution. I hope that the Nobel Prize will help us achieve this goal.

The political and economic problems facing Poland's new non-communist government in 1989 were very serious. Tadeusz Mazoviechi, the new prime minister, was an old friend of Walesa's and a fellow Solidarity member. Walesa, however, disagreed with many of the policies of the new government and of the president, who was a communist. In 1990 the constitution was revised giving the president more power. Walesa ran for the presidency and won becoming the first non-communist president of modern Poland.

*See page 77 for Listening Exercise 7.*

# Albert Schweitzer

### (1875 — 1965)
Alsatian minister, musician, philospher, doctor, and medical missionary

*Awarded the Nobel Peace Prize in 1952 for his life of service to humanity.*

# Albert Schweitzer

Albert Schweitzer was a doctor of philosophy, theology, music, and medicine. His name is synonymous with humanitarianism because he is known throughout the world for his service to humanity and reverence for all life—plant, animal, and human.

He was born on January 14, 1875, in Kayersburg, Alsace, which was part of Germany and later part of France after World War I. He was a sensitive young boy—sensitive to nature, to music, and to the feelings of those around him. He excelled in his academic studies and in music. At the age of twenty-one, young Schweitzer began to question his right to have such a fortunate life without doing something in return for those less fortunate. He made a secret promise to himself that he would continue studying and living for himself until he was thirty; then for the rest of his life he would be of direct service to humanity.

Schweitzer followed in his father's footsteps and was a minister. By the age of thirty he had also established himself as an author, a lecturer, and a musician. He desired to preach the gospel of love through work as well as words, to use his hands as well as his mind. It was at this time that he learned of the great need of medical doctors in the Congo region of Africa. He decided to become a doctor of medicine, and even though his family and friends were surprised and upset about his decision, he entered medical school at the University of Strasbourg Germany.

Medical school took six years. After Schweitzer passed his medical exams, he completed a year of internship at a hospital and took a course in tropical medicine. He was thirty-seven when he was finally prepared to begin his life of service to the sick in the African Congo. Before he left for Africa, Schweitzer married Helen Bresslau, a university professor's daughter who had taken a nursing course so that she could help her future husband in Africa.

On Easter Day, 1913, Dr. and Mrs. Schweitzer sailed for West Africa with boxes of equipment and medicines donated by friends who wanted to help establish a hospital at the Lambaréné Mission in Africa. The morning after the Schweitzers arrived, patients suffering from sleeping sickness, malaria, heart trouble, dysentery, leprosy, injuries, and accidents came to be helped. The Schweitzers treated their patients from an old henhouse, but it was not long before a new hospital building was built with the help and the trust of the African people.

Their work was interrupted by World War I. The Schweitzers, being German citizens in a French colony in Africa, were sent to a prison camp in France. In 1924 Dr. Schweitzer was finally able to return to Lambaréné to rebuild the hospital. Mrs. Schweitzer remained behind in Europe with their young daughter, Rhenna.

When Mrs. Schweitzer returned to Africa in 1929, the hospital at Lambaréné had grown extensively, and there was a well-equipped operating room and a growing staff of doctors and nurses. It was very different from the beginning days when Dr. and Mrs. Schweitzer treated patients in the henhouse.

In 1953 Dr. Schweitzer was awarded the Nobel Peace Prize. He was grateful but said, "No man has the right to pretend that he has worked enough for the cause of peace or declare himself satisfied."

On the morning of September 4, 1965, in his ninetieth year, Dr. Schweitzer died. He was buried next to his wife in a simple grave at Lambaréné.

Dr. Albert Schweitzer chose to live by a philosophy that he called "the reverence for life." In one of his books, *Out of My Life and Thought*, he wrote:

> A man is ethical only when life, as such, is sacred to him, that of plants and animals as well as that of his fellow men, and when he devotes himself helpfully to all life that is in need of help.

*See page 81 for Listening Exercise 8.*

# Andrei D. Sakharov

(1921 — 1989)

Soviet physicist, professor, and human rights activist

*Awarded the Nobel Peace Prize in 1975 for his commitment and work for peace.*

21

# Andrei D. Sakharov

Andrei Sakharov was a Soviet physicist and human rights activist. He was born in Moscow on May 21, 1921.

In 1942 Sakharov graduated from Moscow University and later from the Lebedev Institute of Physics in 1947 with a Ph.D. in physics. During World War II, he was an engineer in a war plant, and from 1948 until 1956, he worked in weapons research. He was an important contributor to the Soviet Union's development of nuclear weapons and is often referred to as "the father of the hydrogen bomb." For his outstanding contributions, the Soviet government awarded him three Orders of Socialist Labor, the Soviet Union's highest civilian award. He was also elected a full member to the Academy of Sciences in 1953, another honor in Sakharov's career as a scientist.

The Soviet leaders were proud of Sakharov and his accomplishments because he was a Russian who was educated only in Soviet schools and therefore an example of the best of the Soviet educational system.

Then, only four years after the first test of the power and effects of the Soviet hydrogen bomb in 1953, Sakharov began to speak out against nuclear weapons. He had realized the impact of radioactive contamination and the potential international danger of nuclear weapons.

He became an embarrassment for the Soviet Union. How could "the father of the hydrogen bomb" now be speaking out against nuclear weapons? Sakharov also criticized his government's suppression of freedom and the individual personality. He published his first book, *Progress, Coexistence, and Intellectual Freedom*, in 1968. In this book he pleaded for international cooperation to share the benefits of scientific progress and to avoid a nuclear catastrophe. He warned the world about polluting the environment, and he criticized the Soviet government's position on human rights.

In 1970 Sakharov helped to establish the Moscow Human Rights Committee. He publicly criticized the Soviet government's treatment of his colleagues and friends who had been punished and imprisoned for expressing opinions which were different from those of the government. Sakharov and the Committee also spoke out against the Soviet policy of denying a Soviet citizen the right to emigrate to another country. The Soviet government punished Sakharov by not allowing him to continue his scientific work.

Sakharov's voice was being heard, and the importance of his message was recognized—if not in his own country, then around the world. In 1974 he received the Eleanor Roosevelt Peace Award, and in 1975 he was awarded the Nobel Peace Prize for his work for human rights. The Soviet government, however, prevented Sakharov from travelling to Oslo, Norway, to accept his prize. Then finally, in January of 1985, he was arrested, his Soviet honors were taken from him, and he was exiled from Moscow to Gorky.

The Soviet government tried to silence Sakharov, but his message has reached around the world. He said:

> The reality of the contemporary world is complex with many planes. It is a fantastic mix of tragedy, irreparable misfortune, apathy, prejudices, and ignorance, plus dynamism, selflessness, hope, and intelligence. The future may be even more tragic. Or it may be more worthy of human beings—better and more intelligent. Or, again, it may not be at all. It depends on all of us . . . in every country of the world. It depends on our wisdom, our freedom from illusion and prejudices, our readiness to work, to practice intelligent austerity and on our kindness and our breadth as human beings.

So even if Sakharov's own country did not at that time recognize the value and intelligence of his contributions to the world, the Nobel Prize Committee recognized Sakharov as "one of the great champions of human rights in our age."

In 1988 and 1989 as the great changes occurred in the Soviet Union, Sakharov was "rehabilitated." He returned from Gorky and spoke out in favor of the Gorbachev reforms. He was elected to the new, more democratic parliament where he was one of the leading spokesmen for change and justice. He died suddenly on December 15, 1989, and was publicly and officially mourned by the entire nation, led by President Gorbachev.

*See page 85 for Listening Exercise 9.*

# Naguib Mahfouz

(1911 —     )

Egyptian writer

*Awarded the 1988 Nobel Prize in Literature. The Nobel Committee stated that Mahfouz "has formed an Arabic narrative art that applies to all mankind."*

24

# Naguib Mahfouz

Naguib Mahfouz is to Arabic literature what Mark Twain was to American literature, "an original with a deep feeling for his people." His writing, although deeply Egyptian and Arabic, has a universal appeal.

Naguib Mahfouz was born in 1911 in Cairo, Egypt (the exact date of his birth is not known). He was the youngest of seven children. As a teenager he was an avid reader and moviegoer. He began writing when he was seventeen and was a student of philosophy and language in high school. In 1930 he entered the University of Cairo. During this time, he published his first article and continued to enjoy writing other articles and short stories. His interest in literature grew, and some of his favorite authors were Tolstoy, Dostoevsky, Chekhov, and Proust. He received his B.A. degree in 1934 and was enrolled in a master's degree program in philosophy, but he chose instead to pursue his love of writing and dropped out of the program. He published his first collection of short stories in 1938, *A Whisper of Madness*.

In 1939, Mahfouz began working in the Ministry of Religious Affairs. He worked there for fifteen years and continued to write. Some of his well-known novels published during this time were: *Games of Fate*, *Khan al-Khalili*, and *New Cairo*. Then in 1956, *Between Two Palaces* was published. This was the book that made Mahfouz famous, and it became the most popular novel in the Arabic language. It is about a Cairo family from the end of World War I to 1944. It has recently been published for the first time in English, and the new title is *Palace Walk*. It is the first volume of a trilogy. The other two volumes are *The Palace of Desire* and *The Sugar Bowl*. The trilogy took eleven years to complete—one year for research, six years to write, and four years to put into print. Time is a constant theme in his novels. Mahfouz says that "the hero of *Palace Walk* is time . . . everything changes because of time."

For many years the Arab world has thought of Naguib Mahfouz as its greatest living novelist. In 1988 Mahfouz was internationally recognized when he was awarded the Nobel Prize in Literature. The Nobel Committee stated that he "has formed an Arabic narrative art that applies to all mankind."

When Mahfouz was asked about the importance of the Nobel Prize to Egypt and the Arab world, he replied:

It's given me for the first time in my life the feeling that my literature could be on the international level. Egypt and the Arab world also get the Nobel Prize with me. I believe that from now on the international doors have opened and in the future, literate people will look for Arab literature, and Arab literature deserves that recognition.

Mahfouz has written over thirty novels. Those published in English include: *Palace Walk, Wedding Song, The Thief and the Dogs,* and *The Beginning and the End.* Some of his work has been criticized by Muslim fundamentalists, and his life has been threatened by them. Nevertheless, he continues to write and live in Agouza, a suburb of Cairo, with his wife and two daughters.

*See page 89 for Listening Exercise 10.*

# Bertrand Arthur William Russell

(1872 — 1970)

British philosopher, mathematician, logician, professor, and social activist

*Awarded the Nobel Prize in Literature in 1950*
*"in recognition of his varied and significant writings,*
*in which he champions humanitarian ideals*
*and freedom of thought."*

# Bertrand Arthur William Russell

Bertrand Russell is considered to be one of the most influential philosophical thinkers and writers of the 20th century.

He was born on May 18, 1872, in Trelleck, Wales. His parents died when he was very young, and he lived with his paternal grandparents at Pembroke Lodge in Richmond Park, Surrey, England. His grandfather was Prime Minister of Great Britain twice, but it was his grandmother who was the most important influence on his social and political conscience. In his autobiography, Russell writes:

> Her fearlessness, her public spirit, her contempt for convention, and her indifference to the opinion of the majority have always seemed good to me and have impressed themselves upon me as worthy of imitation.

He was tutored at home until he was almost sixteen. He was an excellent student and excelled in mathematics. From 1890 until 1894, he attended Trinity College, Cambridge University, and remained there as a fellow from 1895 to 1901 and then as a lecturer from 1910 to 1916.

While at Cambridge, he collaborated with Alfred North Whitehead (a Cambridge professor) on what was to become one of Russell's most important works, *Principia Mathematica*. It consists of three volumes and was written from 1910 through 1913. The basis of the work shows that the concepts of mathematics may be defined with the vocabulary of logic. *Principia Mathematic* established Bertrand Russell as one of the founding fathers of modern analytical philosophy. Both logicians and philosophers of mathematics considered it to be the most important work on logic in the 20th century.

Russell was, however, dismissed from Cambridge because of his association with controversial causes such as socialism, opposition to Britain's involvement in World War I, and pacifism. In 1918 the British government imprisoned him for his pacifistic activities.

He continued to be politically active and controversial throughout his ninety-seven years. In 1955, Bertrand Russell and Albert Einstein wrote the Russell-Einstein Manifesto—a public declaration to people and governments of the world about the necessity of avoiding war and potential nuclear catastrophe. A week before Einstein died, the Manifesto was signed by Russell, Einstein, and eight other world-renowned scientists including Frédéric Joliot-Curie. In 1958, Russell founded the Campaign for Nuclear Disarmament. During the Cuban Missile Crisis, in 1962, he sent letters to U.S. President John F. Kennedy and Soviet Premier Nikita S. Khruschev pleading with them to meet and discuss disarmament. He protested the U.S. military involvement in Vietnam and, with French writer/philosopher Jean Paul Sartre, organized the Vietnam War Crimes Tribunal in Stockholm, Sweden.

Through the turbulent years of his life, Bertrand Russell remained a prolific and well-respected writer in many fields, including logic, mathematics, social philosophy, politics, and even short works of fiction. In 1950 he was awarded the Nobel Prize for Literature "in recognition of his varied and significant writings, in which he champions humanitarian ideals and freedom of thought." Looking back on his life, he wrote:

Three passions, simple but overwhelmingly strong, have governed my life: the longing for love, the search for knowledge and unbearable pity for the suffering of mankind . . . this has been my life. I have found it worth living, and would gladly live it again if the chance were offered me."

*See page 93 for Listening Exercise 11.*

# Gabriel José Garciá Márquez

(1928 —        )

Colombian journalist, novelist, and short story writer

*Awarded the 1982 Nobel Prize in Literature "for his novels and short stories, in which the fantastic and realistic are combined in a richly composed world of imagination, reflecting a continent's life and conflicts."*

# Gabriel José Garciá Márquez

Gabriel Garciá Márquez is an outstanding Colombian novelist and short-story writer. He is an extraordinary storyteller who combines fantasy and reality. He says that the most important figure in his life was his grandfather, a retired army officer who told many long tales about his war days.

Today, Garciá Márquez carries on the fine tradition of story-telling and says that he is not concerned with morals or messages in his stories—only in reporting the behavior of his characters. He says, "The writer is not here to make declarations, but to tell about things."

His own parents were too poor to raise Gabriel, so he grew up in the large, gloomy house of his maternal grandparents. He was the oldest of twelve children and was born on March 6, 1928 in the village of Aracataca near the northern Caribbean coast of Colombia. His grandmother, who was interested in ghosts, spirits, and dead ancestors, loved to tell stories about strange and supernatural happenings. It is clear in the writing of Garciá Márquez that his grandparents made a big impression on him and encouraged his imagination.

When Gabriel was eight years old, he left his grandparents' house to go to school at the National Secondary School of Zipaquirá, near the capital of Colombia, Bogotá. After he graduated in 1946, he studied law at the University of Bogotá. He studied law for five years but never really liked it, so he never finished his degree.

Starting in 1948, there was a period of violence in Colombia which lasted on and off for about ten years. Two hundred thousand people died. It was during this time that Garciá Márquez wrote his first three books about what was happening in his country. Afterwards, he studied journalism and in 1950 began to write for the daily paper *El Heraldo* in the town of Barranqilla. He did not earn much money, but he developed as a writer. He was influenced by the writings of Faulkner, Hemingway, Woolf, Kafka, and Joyce.

In 1954 he returned to Bogotá to be a film critic and reporter for the newspaper *El Espectador*. He wrote a series of articles about what really happened in the disaster of a Colombian naval ship. The dictator of Colombia, Gustavo Rojas Pinilla, was embarrassed and angry. The articles, however, made Garciá Márquez famous and were later published as a book. The newspaper sent him on assignment to Rome and Paris, but while he was in Paris, the paper was shut down by the Colombian government. He remained in Paris for several years and then moved to Caracas, Venezuela. He never stopped writing, even though making a living was a struggle.

In 1959 he began working as a journalist for the official press agency of Fidel Castro's Cuba, first in Bogotá, Colombia, and later in New York City. After taking a trip through Faulkner country to New Orleans, Garciá Márquez left his job and moved to Mexico City, Mexico. From 1961 to 1965 he did not write any fiction; he worked as a screenwriter, editor, and copywriter. Then one day in 1965, he began to write his masterpiece.

*One Hundred Years of Solitude* was first published in 1967 in Buenos Aires, Argentina. It was a huge success and sold over one million copies in Spanish. It was then translated into at least twenty different languages and sold in more than twenty-five countries. Critics say it is a modern masterpiece. In writing this book, Garciá Márquez perfected his unique style that is very different from his early work when he was a journalist. The images are rich, detailed, and imaginative. It is like reading a dream, and the dream has its own logic and reality. It is because of this that his style of writing is described as surrealistic, the definition of which is "having the intense irrational reality of a dream." Garciá Márquez explains that "surrealism comes from the reality of Latin America."

The story of *One Hundred Years of Solitude* is about love and death, war and peace, youth and age, in over six generations of Buendiá family who live in the fictional town of Macondo where strange and supernatural things happen. Some say the story is really about the history of Latin America. The Nobel Prize-winning Chilean poet, Pablo Neruda, says that the book is "perhaps the greatest revelation in the Spanish language since the *Don Quixote* of Cervantes."

In 1982 Gabriel Garciá Márquez was awarded the Nobel Prize in Literature. The Nobel Committee said that he was awarded the Prize "for his novels and short stories, in which the fantastic and the realistic are combined in a richly composed world of imagination, reflecting a continent's life and conflicts."

*See page 97 for Listening Exercise 11.*

# Pearl S. Buck

(1892 — 1973)

American author and humanitarian

*Awarded the Nobel Prize in Literature in 1938 "for her rich and genuine epic pictures of Chinese life and for her masterly biographies."*

33

# Pearl S. Buck

Pearl S. Buck was an American novelist, humanitarian, and China's most famous, unofficial, Western interpreter.

She was born on June 26, 1892, in her mother's family home in the small town of Hillsboro, West Virginia. She was the fifth of seven children born to missionary parents Absalom and Caroline Sydenstricker. Three of the children died from tropical diseases, and Pearl grew up as the eldest daughter.

When Pearl was five months old, her family sailed for China. She was raised in the two worlds of East and West. Her beloved Chinese nurse, Wang Amah, cared for the young Pearl and was like her mother and teacher in the Chinese world. Pearl writes in her autobiography, *My Several Worlds*:

> Thus I grew up in a double world, the small white clean Presbyterian American world of my parents and the big loving not-too-clean Chinese world, and there was no communication between them. When I was in the Chinese world, I was Chinese, I spoke Chinese and behaved as a Chinese and ate as the Chinese did, and I shared their thoughts and feelings. When I was in the American world, I shut the door between.

She began writing in 1922, and in her many books, essays, articles, and short stories, Pearl Buck opened the door between these two worlds. Throughout her writings the conflicts between East and West, old and new, are examined and explored.

Her first published novel was *East Wind: West Wind* (1930), a story about the contrasts between Eastern and Western civilizations. In 1931, her second and most well-known novel, *The Good Earth*, was published. This was the novel that changed Pearl Buck's life. The story was a realistic, sympathetic portrayal of a Chinese peasant family—the hardships, the struggles, the joys, and the sadness—the human reality that reached beyond the geographic and cultural boundaries. It was the first time the door of the mysterious Orient was opened wide and the Western world invited in. The book was awarded the Pulitzer Prize in 1932. It was on the best-seller list for months; it sold almost two million copies, was translated into over thirty languages, was adapted for a Broadway play, and made into an award-winning Hollywood film.

Pearl continued to write about China in *Sons* and *A House Divided*. She later wrote two biographies of her parents, *The Exile* and *Fighting Angel*. It was for these early works that she was awarded the 1938 Nobel Prize in Literature. It was the first time an American woman had received a Nobel Prize in Literature. The Swedish Academy said during the award ceremony:

> By awarding this year's Prize to Pearl Buck for the notable works which pave the way to a human sympathy passing over widely separated racial boundaries and for the studies of human ideals . . . the Swedish Academy feels that it acts in harmony and accord with the aim of Alfred Nobel's dream for the future.

Pearl Buck continued to write until the time of her death on March 6, 1973, in Danby, Vermont. The variety of themes included: the conflict between work and marriage, women's rights, racism, interracial marriage, development of the atomic bomb, her experiences as a mother of a retarded daughter, and widowhood.

She was a very productive writer, and by the end of her eighty-one years she had written over one hundred books, as well as countless speeches, articles, and scripts.

Her writing, however, was not the only way that she expressed her concerns for global understanding and freedom for all people. In her personal life she was the mother of ten children, only one of whom was her natural daughter. The other nine were her adopted children of different nationalities. In 1949 she established Welcome House, which was an adoption agency for Asian Americans. Later, in 1964, she founded the Pearl S. Buck Foundation to assist fatherless, and often stateless, half-American children throughout Asia.

Pearl Buck's literary and humanitarian contributions made her a respected world figure. Her insights about China are still very appropriate today in the face of China's social and political turmoil. She said in 1938 in her Nobel Prize acceptance speech:

> The minds of my own country and of China, my foster country, are alike in many ways, but above all, alike in our common love of freedom. And today more than ever, this is true, now when China's whole being is engaged in the greatest of all struggles, the struggle for

freedom. I have never admired China more than I do now when I see her uniting as she has never before, against the enemy who threatens her freedom. With this determination for freedom, which is in so profound a sense the essential quality in her nature, I know she is unconquerable.

*See page 101 for Listening Exercise 13.*

# Paul Anthony Samuelson

## (1915 —      )

### American professor of economics

*Awarded the 1970 Nobel Prize in Economics for doing "more than any other contemporary economist to raise the level of scientific analysis in economic theory."*

# Paul Anthony Samuelson

Paul Samuelson was born on May 15, 1915, in Gary, Indiana. He was educated at the University of Chicago in Illinois, where he received his B.S. degree in 1935. He continued his studies at Harvard University in Massachusetts and received his M.A. in 1936 and his Ph.D. in 1941. He is Institute Professor of Economics at the Massachusetts Institute of Technology.

In 1947 Samuelson wrote *Foundations of Economic Analysis* in which he used the language of mathematics to explain the world of economics. In 1948 he wrote *Economics* which is considered to be the most successful and influential economics text of our time. *Economics* is still being published in new, revised editions today.

Samuelson was awarded the 1970 Nobel Prize in Economics for doing "more than any other contemporary economist to raise the level of scientific analysis in economic theory."

In addition, Samuelson wrote a regular column for *Newsweek* magazine and is considered to be one of the world's most respected economists. He is unlike many economists because he "accepts the fact that in a democracy, public choice, rather than theory or ideology, will determine economic policy." He considers himself to be a liberal and, therefore, concerned with improvements in living standards and reductions in inequality. He says:

> My own concern is with improvements in living standards, not with expansion in bureaucrats' power. Reductions in inequality of condition and opportunity matter more than fulfillment of five-year plans or realization of programs for social reconstruction.

In economics there are three languages that may be used. Samuelson insists that mathematics is a language and prefers using it to explain and solve economic problems. An example using the three different languages to explain the same thing follows:

### Mathematics

$$c = f(y)$$

| | | |
|---|---|---|
| c = consumption | y = income | f = function |

## Economese
consumption function
or
propensity-to-consume schedule

## English
The more we earn, the more we spend; but as our incomes rise,
we increase our spending less and less and increase
our saving more and more.

Samuelson, who has six children, says:

> I think having children is the biggest kick in life . . . but aside from that, the greatest pleasure I have—the greatest personal pleasure—is in the puzzle-solving aspect of economics, the mathematical work. But in the end, the puzzle is a much better puzzle if it isn't just a puzzle, if it has relevance to real-world problems.

Samuelson's life work has been to use economics in the service of humanity. He is a pioneer in the "reconstruction of economics into a coherent and orderly discipline. He has done more than anyone of his time to disseminate its insights and to influence government policy at the highest level."

*See page 107 for Listening Exercise 14.*

# Milton Friedman

## (1912 —        )

### American professor of economics

*Awarded the 1976 Nobel Prize in Economics because it is
"very rare for an economist to wield such influence,
directly or indirectly, not only on the direction of
scientific research but also on
the actual practice."*

# Milton Friedman

Milton Friedman was born on July 31, 1912 in Brooklyn, New York. He was educated at Rutgers University in New Jersey and received his B.A. degree in 1932. He attended the University of Chicago in Illinois and received his M.A. degree in 1933. In 1946, he received his Ph.D. from Columbia University in New York.

He is considered to be America's best-known conservative economist. He is a champion of the free-market and one of the most effective defenders of capitalism in America. Friedman is most famous for his work on money and a new kind of economics that he introduced called "monetarism." Monetarism challenged the thinking of most economists, including Paul A. Samuelson, Friedman's contemporary. Simply stated, Friedman believes that the role of monetary policy (the regulation by the Federal Reserve System of the nation's money supply and interest rates) plays a bigger part than previously thought in the level of economic activity and the price level.

In his book *Capitalism and Freedom* (1962), Friedman discusses the role of competitive capitalism: "the organization of the bulk of economic activity through private enterprise operating in a free market— as a system of economic freedom and a necessary condition for political freedom." He further states that he believes that the government's role in the free enterprise system should be very limited—a belief that makes him popular with industry and businessmen and different from leading contemporary economists who look for ways to use government to improve the performance of economy and to advance social welfare. He further advocates a decentralization of governmental power:

> The preservation of freedom is the protective reason for limiting and decentralizing governmental power. But there is also a constructive reason. The great advances of civilization, whether in architecture or painting, in science or literature, in industry or agriculture, have never come from centralized government. . . . Newton and Leibnitz; Einstein and Bohr; Shakespeare, Milton, and Pasternak; Whitney, McCormick, Edison, and Ford; Jane Addams, Florence Nightingale, and Albert Schweitzer; no one of these opened new frontiers in

human knowledge and understanding, in literature, in technical possibilities, or in the relief of human misery in response to governmental directives. Their achievements were the product of individual genius, of strongly held minority views, of a social climate permitting variety and diversity. Government can never duplicate the variety and diversity of individual action. At any moment in time, by imposing uniform standards in housing, or nutrition, or clothing, government could undoubtedly improve the level of living of many individuals. . . . But in the process, government would replace progress by stagnation, it would substitute uniform mediocrity for the variety essential for that experimentation. . . ."

Friedman says that capitalism is a prerequisite for human freedom, that the combination of capitalism and freedom brings a hope of a better world. Capitalism does not, however, guarantee a free state. In fact, there are many countries in the world today with capitalistic economies where civil liberties are denied daily. Friedman admits that it is possible for a country to be economically capitalistic and yet not politically free.

In 1976, Milton Friedman was awarded the Nobel Prize in Economics, and the Nobel Committee noted his book *Capitalism and Freedom* and added that it is "very rare for an economist to wield such influence, directly or indirectly, not only on the direction of scientific research but also on the actual practice." His theories have influenced economists and policymakers in the United States and the world.

*See page 111 for Listening Exercise 15.*

# Michael Stuart Brown

(1941 —      )

# Joseph Leonard Goldstein

(1940 —      )

American medical doctors and molecular geneticists

*Awarded the 1985 Nobel Prize in Medicine for the research that has "revolutionized our knowledge about the regulation of cholesterol metabolism and the treatment of diseases caused by abnormally elevated cholesterol levels in the blood."*

# Michael Stuart Brown and Joseph Leonard Goldstein

Michael Stuart Brown was born in New York City, New York, on April 13, 1941. He received both his B.A. and M.D. degrees from the University of Pennsylvania.

Joseph Leonard Goldstein was born on April 18, 1940, in Sumter, South Carolina. He received his B.S. degree in 1962 from Washington and Lee University in Lexington, Virginia. Then, in 1966, he received his M.D. degree from Southwestern Medical School, University of Texas in Dallas.

Dr. Brown and Dr. Goldstein met in 1966 when they were both interns and later residents at Massachusetts General Hospital in Boston. They became close friends. In 1968, after residency, they both joined the staff of the National Institute of Health in Bethesda, Maryland, to gain experience in research. Dr. Goldstein's research focused on the genetic aspects of heart disease. Dr. Brown's research was primarily on the role of enzymes in the chemistry of the digestive system. In 1971, Dr. Brown continued his research as a research fellow at the University of Texas Health Science Center in Dallas. It was here that he began studying the role of an enzyme that controls cholesterol production. A year later, Dr. Goldstein joined the Center as head of the medical school's first department of medical genetics. The focus of his work was to try to understand the basic defect in the genetic disease, FHC or familial hypercholesterolemia. FHC was first identified as a genetic disease in 1939, by Carl Müller of Oslo, Norway. Müller found that a genetic defect caused the condition which resulted in high blood cholesterol levels and heart attacks, sometimes in very young people. And so, Dr. Brown and Dr. Goldstein worked together to try to understand the cholesterol problem.

To understand the importance of their research it is necessary to know some facts about cholesterol. There are two sources of cholesterol, the body's liver and fat in food. Cholesterol is essential to the life of cells, which take in cholesterol from the blood. Lipoproteins carry cholesterol throughout the bloodstream. There are low-density lipoproteins (L.D.L.) and high-density lipoproteins (H.D.L.). L.D.L. cholesterol is "bad" and may be the cause of health problems. H.D.L. is the "good" cholesterol because it takes the L.D.L. away from the linings of the arteries where it likes to collect, clogging the arteries and causing heart disease. Coronary heart disease kills more people in the Western world than any other disease, and atherosclerosis, hardening of the arteries, kills one million Americans each year.

So, what Dr. Brown and Dr. Goldstein found was that cells make L.D.L. receptors that take in cholesterol from the blood and that people with FHC don't have enough L.D.L. receptors. Dr. Goldstein said, "Our work has pointed to the importance of this receptor in control of blood cholesterol and how the receptor can be raised through drugs and a low-cholesterol, low-fat diet." If a person eats food high in cholesterol, then more of the "bad" cholesterol flows through the bloodstream, more is available to the cells, fewer L.D.L. receptors form to absorb cholesterol and so more cholesterol collects on the arterial walls and blocks blood to the heart.

The 1985 Nobel Prize in Physiology or Medicine was awarded to Dr. Brown and Dr. Goldstein. The Nobel Committee stated that their research has "revolutionized our knowledge about the regulation of cholesterol metabolism and the treatment of diseases caused by abnormally elevated cholesterol levels in the blood."

*See page 115 for Listening Exercise 13.*

# Albert Einstein

## (1879 — 1955)

German, later Swiss and American, theoretical physicist and
university professor

*Awarded the Nobel Prize in Physics in 1921 for his theory
of the photoelectric effect (not for his theory of relativity
because it was still too controversial at the time).*

# Albert Einstein

It is generally thought that Albert Einstein was the greatest theoretical physicist who has ever lived. His ideas and theories changed the world. Some of his major contributions in physics were the theory of relativity ($E=mc^2$), quantum theory, and statistical physics. He was also a scientific philosopher and pacifist.

Albert Einstein was born on March 14, 1879, in Ulm, Germany. His interest in science began when he was only five years old. His father had given him a magnetic compass, and the young Albert wondered about the unseen forces that made the compass needle point north.

In school, Albert was not a very good student. When his father went to speak with the schoolmaster about what profession his son should choose, the schoolmaster replied that it did not matter because Albert Einstein would never make a success of anything. Albert dropped out of school at fifteen because he hated strict discipline and rote learning. He loved playing the violin and mathematics.

When his family moved to Milan, Italy, Albert decided he wanted to study physics at the Swiss Federal Institute of Technology in Zürich, Switzerland. His father tried to convince him to forget this "philosophical nonsense" and take up the "sensible trade" of electrical engineering. Albert, however, had other plans.

He failed the Institute's entrance exam, but after a year's study at a school near Zürich he passed and entered in 1896. He graduated in 1900. He was unable to get a university teaching position, so he became a private physics and mathematics tutor for two years. During this time, he renounced his German citizenship and became a Swiss citizen on February 21, 1901. He maintained his Swiss citizenship throughout his life. He was proud of it because he thought Switzerland was a country of cultural diversity, political and religious tolerance, and personal freedom.

In 1902 Einstein took a job in the Swiss Patent Office in Bern. The work was not very demanding so he had plenty of time to develop his theories that would later change science forever. He married Mileva Maric (a former classmate at the Institute) in 1903, and they had two sons, Hans Albert and Edward. In 1909, at the age of thirty, Einstein finally left his job at the Patent Office and began his lifelong career in the academic world. His genius had begun to be recognized, and by 1914 he was at the top of his profession as a member of the Royal Prussian Academy of Sciences in Berlin. In 1921 he was awarded the Nobel Prize in physics. Because Einstein's theories were shaking the scientific world and society, their validity was often challenged, researched, and debated by others. He was awarded the Nobel Prize for his theory of the photoelectric effect and not for his better-known theory of relativity ($E=mc^2$) because too few scientists could fully comprehend it. Simply stated, it means that (m) matter and (e) energy are the same things only in different forms. This idea, however, revolutionized the accepted perception of the physical universe.

In 1933, when Adolf Hitler came into power, Einstein and his second wife, his cousin Elsa, moved to Princeton, New Jersey. He became a professor at the Institute for Advanced Study where he remained until his death on April 18, 1955. During these latter years he became interested in Zionism—the preservation of Jewish heritage and the establishment of a Jewish homeland. He was a pacifist, and shortly before his death he wrote and signed the Russell-Einstein Manifesto, which warned the people and governments of the world about the potential of nuclear catastrophe.

Albert Einstein is remembered as the greatest scientist in the world, the absent-minded professor, a Zionist, a pacifist, and a wise man. Einstein was often misunderstood by his contemporaries, but this is often the case with genius—it is not fully recognized in the time that it appears. Einstein could have been writing about himself when he wrote this about his friend the controversial British philosopher and writer, Bertrand Russell:

> Great spirits have always encountered violent opposition from mediocre minds. The mediocre mind is incapable of understanding the man who refuses to bow blindly to conventional prejudices and chooses instead to express his opinions courageously and honestly.

*See page 119 for Listening Exercise 17.*

# Irène Joliot-Curie

(1897 — 1956)

# Frédéric Joliot-Curie

(1900 — 1958)

French chemists

*Awarded the 1935 Nobel Prize in Chemistry "for their jointly performed synthesis of new radioactive elements."*

# Irène and Frédéric Joliot-Curie

Irène Joliot-Curie was born on September 12, 1897, in Paris, France. Her famous parents, Marie and Pierre Curie, had dedicated their lives to the scientific research of radioactive elements. The Curies had discovered two radioactive elements: polonium and radium. In 1903 they were jointly awarded the Nobel Prize in Physics for the discovery of radium. Pierre Curie died in 1906, but Marie Curie continued their work, and in 1911 she was awarded the Nobel Prize again, this time in Chemistry, for isolating the element of radium. Marie Curie was the first woman to be awarded a Nobel Prize in Physics or Chemistry and her daughter, Irène, became the second.

Irène grew up in the world of science. After she graduated from the University of Paris, she began to work at her parent's laboratory, the Curie Institute of Radium, in Paris. She met Frédéric Joliot when he came to work on the staff of researchers.

Frédéric Joliot was born on March 19, 1900, in Paris, France. He was well-educated even though his parents did not have a lot of money. He also graduated from the University of Paris and in 1925 began working at the Curie Institute. A year later, Irène and Frédéric were married, on October 4, 1926.

They decided to hyphenate their last names to symbolize that they worked together in an equal partnership and to carry on the Curie name. Irène was shy and serious; Frédéric was gregarious and loved to talk. They complemented each other and made an excellent team. Together they raised their children, Hélène and Pierre, and together they worked many long hours in the laboratory.

Their discovery of radioactive artificial isotopes earned them the 1935 Nobel Prize in Chemistry. Marie Curie died only a few weeks before this honor was awarded to her daughter. Marie Curie died of a condition in which the bone marrow fails to make the necessary red blood cells. It was caused by the years of exposure to radiation in the laboratory.

Irène and Frédéric had been working on changing stable elements into radioactive ones, and for the first time a way had been found to release by artificial means some of the energy that Albert Einstein had shown to exist in every atom of matter.

The Curies and the Joliot-Curies were good friends with Albert Einstein. In 1955, when Einstein and Bertrand Russell wrote the Russell-Einstein Manifesto, Frédéric Joliot-Curie was among the nine other famous scientists who signed it. The conclusion of the Manifesto states:

> In view of the fact that in any future war nuclear weapons will certainly be employed, and that any such weapons threaten the continued existence of mankind, we urge the governments of the world to realize, and to acknowledge publicly, that their purpose cannot be furthered by a world war, and we urge them, consequently, to find peaceful means for the settlement of all matters of dispute between them.

The Joliot-Curies wer very much aware of their social responsibility as scientists. They belonged to the World Federation of Associations of Scientific Workers, an organization dedicated to utilizing science as a means of solving problems and benefitting society. Frédéric stated, "French science does not want to have anything to do with atomic research other than for peace. All our efforts are being utilized in the development of this tremendous energy for the advancement of humanity." He said this when he was the High-Commissioner of France's first Atomic Energy Commission.

After full and rewarding personal and professional lives, Irène and Frédéric Joliot-Curie died within two years of each other. Irène died on March 17, 1956, of leukemia. Leukemia is a form of cancer which can be caused by x-ray or radiation exposure. Frédéric died on August 14, 1958, of liver and intestinal problems, also due to radiation exposure.

It is sadly ironic that the scientific research that Marie Curie and the Joliot-Curies had devoted their lives to eventually caused their deaths. The Joliot-Curie radioactive isotopes have been further developed and are used today in many beneficial ways, including the diagnosis and treatment of diseases such as leukemia, other types of cancer, and thyroid disease. Because of their dedication and sense of responsibility, humanity has benefitted.

*See page 123 for Listening Exercise 18.*

*Actual size.*

The medals are about 2½ inches in diameter.
They are struck in 23-carat gold
worth about 20.000 Swedish Kronor.

## *Listening Exercise 1*

## Alfred Bernhard

# Nobel

*(Reading on page 1)*

## *Key Words*

born
inventor, invented
explosive
contribution
peace
established
prize
mankind
died, death
award, awarded
elected
weapon

# Alfred Bernhard Nobel

Alfred Nobel was _____ on October 21, 1833 in Stockholm, Sweden. He was the third son of Swedish _____ Immanuel Nobel. All three sons worked in their father's business of manufacturing _____. Alfred _____ dynamite, an _____ which is used in the construction of roads, railroads, and canals. He became very wealthy from the sales of his _____.

Nobel thought that his scientific work was his major _____ to world progress, but because of his interest in _____, science, and literature he _____ a fund. He stated that the interest from the fund would be given as _____ to those who provided great benefits for _____. His fund has made the name Nobel well-known throughout the world.

Alfred Nobel _____ on December 10, 1896. A few years after his _____ the Nobel Foundation of Stockholm was _____. The first prizes were _____ in 1901 in the fields of physics, chemistry, physiology or medicine, literature, and _____. In 1969 a _____ in the field of economics was _____ by the Central Bank of Sweden.

The winners in physics, chemistry, and economics are named by the Royal Swedish Academy of Sciences. The physiology or medicine _____ is _____ by the Caroline Institute in Stockholm.

The peace _____ is _____ by a committee of five people _____ by the Norwegian Parliament.

The amount of each _____ has increased from about $30,000 to over $400,000. _____ are _____ each year. If in a certain year a _____ is not _____ in a field, the money is held in the Nobel _____ fund. _____, however, must be _____ every five years. A single _____ may be divided among two or three winners, and it is possible to win twice. The _____ _____ has been _____ to individuals and to organizations such as the International Red Cross and Amnesty International.

It is interesting that the name Nobel is associated with dynamite and _____. Alfred Nobel knew the destructive power of _____, but he was a pacifist at heart. As he once said, "Perhaps if a very terrible _____ of war could be _____, then it would be necessary for nations to turn to _____."

***Peace***

*Three men form a fraternal bond beneath the phrase*
*Pro pace et fraternitate gentium.*
*The laureate's name is engraved*
*on the medal's edge.*

## Listening Exercise 2

### Desmond

# Tutu

*(Reading on page 3)*

## Key Words:
### New

graduated
teacher, teach
entered
theological, theology
received
goal
politician, political
involved, involvement
injustice, just
educational
message
nonviolent
advocate
recognized
courage

### Old

born
die
peace
established
award
prize

# Desmond Tutu

Bishop Desmond Mpilo Tutu was _____ Klerksdorp in the Western Transvaal, which is part of South Africa. Tutu _____ from the University of South Africa in 1954. He was a school _____ from 1955 until 1958, when he _____ St. Peter's _____ College in Rosettenville, Johannesburg. In 1960 he _____ and became a deacon. Between 1962 and 1966 Tutu, with his wife and children, lived in London, England, where he _____ his Master's degree in _____.

Years later, in 1975, Tutu became the first black Dean of the Anglican Church. Then in 1985, he became Johannesburg's first black Anglican Bishop.

Bishop Tutu voices the problems and _____ of many black South Africans. He is not a _____, and yet he is _____ in _____ issues. He says of his _____, "I cannot help it when I see _____. I cannot keep quiet."

He wants equal citizenship for South African blacks, the abolition of the apartheid system, and a common _____ system that will change the quality of South African society.

His _____ includes _____ solutions. He _____ the ideals and principles that Martin Luther King, Jr., _____ for. Tutu has taken a firm stand against the evils of apartheid and is _____ internationally for his _____ and _____ efforts to _____ a democratic and _____ society in South Africa. In 1984 he was _____ the Nobel _____.

Bishop Tutu describes apartheid as being "as evil and as vicious as Nazism and Communism."

He also speaks of the vision of the unification of the black and white communities. He believes that South Africa can _____ the world "what unity in diversity really is about."

*Peace*

*The front of The Peace Prize*
*Alfred Nobel (1833 - 1896)*

*Listening Exercise 3*

Mother

# Teresa

*(Reading on page 5)*

## Key Words:

| *New* | *Old* |
|-------|-------|
| suffering | die |
| poor, poorest | born |
| member | enter |
| dedicate | cstablished |
| service, serve | recognize |
| religious | award |
| dignity | peace |
| founded | prize |
| missionaries | message |
| compassionate | mankind |

# Mother Teresa

Mother Teresa is internationally respected for her work in relieving the _____ of the _____, the abandoned, and the _____.

She was _____ on August 27, 1910, in Skopje, Yugoslavia. She attended a local government school, and as a young student there, she became a _____ of a Catholic association for children. She was only twelve years old when she knew that she wanted to _____ her life to helping others. At the age of eighteen, she _____ the order of the Sisters of Our Lady of Loreto. She taught in the order's schools in Calcutta, India, until September 10, 1946, when she had "the call within a call." This call was her heart telling her that she should help the _____ while living among them.

In February 1948, Mother Teresa was granted special permission from the Vatican to leave the convent "in order to spend herself in the _____ of the _____ and the needy in the slums of Calcutta, and to gather around her some companions ready to undertake the same work." On August 16, 1948, she took off the _____ clothes of the Loreto nun and put on a cheap, simple, white sari with a blue border, a small cross pinned to the left shoulder, and open sandals on her feet. She began her new _____ by bringing _____ people from the streets into a home where they could _____ in _____ and with _____.

Mother Teresa has since _____ many homes for the

_____, orphanages for the hundreds of sick, unwanted, or abandoned children, schools for these children, and leper clinics. She says, "Any work of love brings a person face to face with God."

In 1959, she _____ a Roman Catholic order—the _____ of Charity. These sisters, brothers, and co-workers have committed themselves to _____ the _____ of the _____ all over the world. Mother Teresa served as the head of the order until 1990 when she resigned due to _____ health.

Mother Teresa's _____ _____ was _____ internationally when she was _____ the Nobel _____ _____ in 1979. Her _____ to _____ may be simply stated in her own words: "We can do no great things—only small things with great love.

**Physiology and Medicine**

*The Genius of Medicine holds an open book*
*on her lap, gathering in a bowl*
*the water welling out from a rock*
*in order to allay a sick girl's thirst.*

*Listening Exercise 4*

Elie

# Wiesel

*(Reading on page 7)*

## *Key Words*
### *New*

survivor
inhumane
freed
devoted
tragic
prevent
punishment
recipient
spiritual
leader

### *Old*

born
death, dead
die
teach
message
religion
prize
peace
dignity

# Elie Wiesel

Elie Wiesel is a Jewish novelist, journalist, lecturer, and spokesman for the _____ of the Holocaust—the Nazi effort to destroy the Jewish people during World War II.

He was _____ on September 30, 1928, in Sighet, Romania. Elie was only sixteen when he and his mother, father, and three sisters were sent to the Nazi concentration camp in Auschwitz, Poland.

During the Nazi regime, Jews throughout Europe were sent to concentration camps. These camps were _____ camps. The living conditions were _____. People _____ of illness and starvation, and others were killed in the gas chambers. Approximately six million Jews _____ during the Holocaust. When the war ended in 1945, Elie, his two older sisters, and all the other camp _____ were _____.

Elie Wiesel has _____ his life to being a witness and spokesman. He says that, as a Jew, one must do this. As a Jew, one must be a link between the _____ of the Holocaust and today's world. As a Jew, one must be a link between the Jew and the non-Jew. In his writing and _____ he retells the story of that _____ time in the world's history so that history will not repeat itself. His _____ is that only by remembering can we hope to _____ future holocausts: "Memory may perhaps be our only answer. Our only hope to save the world from ultimate _____, a nuclear holocaust."

Today, he lives in New York City with his wife Marion, her daughter Jennifer, and their son Elisha. He commutes one day a week to Boston, Massachusetts, where he is a professor of _____ at Boston University. He has written over thirty books, and in 1983 he won the International Literary _____ for _____. In 1986 he was the _____ of the Nobel _____ _____. The Nobel Committee said that Elie Wiesel is "one of the most important _____ _____ and guides," and that his _____ is "one of _____, atonement, and _____."

At the World Gathering of Jewish Holocaust _____ in Jerusalem in June 1981, Elie Wiesel, with 7, 000 others, pledged that the Holocaust "must never be forgotten, never be repeated." Never Again.

**Physics and Chemistry**

*Nature in the features of a goddess resembling Isis
emerges from the clouds and holds in her arms
a cornucopia. The veil that covers her face is
held up by the Genius of Science.*

68

# The
# Dalai Lama

*(Reading on page 9)*

## Key Words:
### New

protect
search, searched
claimed
racially, race
exile
cause
honoring
support
expressed

### Old

religion
leader
die
born
mankind
recognize
educate
suffer
award
peace
prize
advocate
free
courage
justice
human
compassion

# The Dalai Lama

The Fourteenth Dalai Lama says of himself, "I am a simple Buddhist monk, no more, no less." But to the people of Tibet, he is their monarch and _____ _____. The title, "Dalai Lama" means "Ocean of Wisdom." The followers of Buddha believe he is the reincarnation of the first "Buddha of Mercy," who appeared in 1391 and whose purpose was and continues to be to _____ all living beings. When one Dalai Lama _____ another is _____ to continue to help _____. To the Tibetans, the Dalai Lama represents the Tibetan way of life.

The Fourteenth Dalai Lama was _____ on June 6, 1935, in the small farming village of Taktser, Tibet. Taktser is about 9,000 feet above the sea, and the people grow wheat and barley. The Dalai Lama was _____ into a large family and lived as a farmer's son until he was four years old.

The Thirteenth Dalai Lama _____ in 1933, and the _____ began for the Fourteenth. The Lamaist monks _____ the many towns and villages of Tibet. They came to Taktser, and after passing several tests the two-year-old son of a farmer was _____ as the Fourteenth Dalai Lama. At the age of four-and-a-half, he was formally _____ and he sat on the Lion Throne in the holy city of Lhasa as the ruler of Tibet. The young Dalai Lama was _____ in the thousand-room Potala Palace overlooking Lhasa. His family did not live in the Palace with him; they lived in a house near the Palace, and he visited them at least once a month.

In 1950, when the Dalai Lama was fifteen, the Chinese Communist armies of Mao Tse-Tung invaded Tibet. The Communists _____ that Tibet was part of China. The Tibetans, however, _____ that _____, culturally, and geographically they were a separate country. In 1959, the Dalai Lama went into _____ in India. The Chinese Communist domination continues today, and the Tibetans continue to _____. The Dalai Lama says:

I would dare say that no people have _____ more since the Second World War; and their _____ have not ended, they are continuing every day, and they will continue until the Chinese leave our country, or until Tibetans have ceased to exist as a _____ or as a _____ community.

The Dalai Lama has tried for over thirty years to keep the world interested in the _____ of Tibet's independence, even though he continues to live in _____ in India.

In 1989, the Dalai Lama was _____ the Nobel _____ _____ for _____ "_____ solutions based upon tolerance and mutual respect in order to preserve the historical and cultural heritage of his people."

_____ the Dalai Lama can be seen as the world's _____ for Tibetan _____. The Dalai Lama himself has _____ his hope in this way:

My hope rests in the _____ of the Tibetans, and the love of truth and _____ which is still in the heart of the _____ _____; and my faith is in the _____ of Lord Buddha.

71

### Literature

*A young man sits under a laurel tree
and, enchanted, listens to and writes
the song of the Muse*

## *Listening Exercise 6*

## Martin Luther

# King, Jr.

*(Reading on page 12)*

## *Key Words*
### *New*

struggle
rights
oppressed
influential, influenced
excellent
arrested
movement
assassination, assassinated

### *Old*

| | |
|---|---|
| peace | member |
| devote | involve |
| poor | contribute |
| race | found |
| lead, leadership | protect |
| born | educate |
| graduate | recipient |
| honor | peace |
| theology | prize |
| receive | support |
| teach, taught | death |
| religion | spiritual |
| nonviolent | free |

# Martin Luther King, Jr.

Dr. Martin Luther King, Jr., was a man of _____ who _____ his life to the _____ for equal civil _____ for the _____, the disadvantaged, and the _____ _____ in the United States. He is considered to be the most _____ civil _____ _____ of the 1950's and 1960's.

King was _____ on January 15, 1929, in Atlanta, Georgia. He was the second of three children, and his father was a Baptist minister. He was an _____ student and _____ from college with _____ at the age of nineteen. Later, in 1951, he _____ first in his class from _____ school, and in 1955 he _____ his Ph.D. in _____.

As a student in _____ school, King studied the life and _____ of Mahatma Gandhi of India. King's own personal and _____ philosophies were strongly _____ by Gandhi. King _____, preached, and practiced Gandhi's doctrine of _____ civil disobedience.

In 1953, King married Coretta Scott and then in 1954 took a job as a Baptist minister in Montgomery, Alabama. Later, in 1955, Rosa Parks, a black woman and _____ of his church, was _____ for refusing to give up her seat on the bus to a white man. This incident started the civil _____ _____ in the United States. King became _____ by organizing a bus boycott in Montgomery. This boycott and others _____ to an important new law when in 1956 the

Supreme Court ruled that segregation on public transportation was illegal.

In 1957 King helped to _____ the Southern Christian _____ Conference whose purpose was to coordinate the many civil _____ organizations. In his work for SCLC, King travelled and spoke in many cities all over the United States. While he was in New York City, in 1958, there was an _____ attempt. However, this did not stop King or the growing civil _____ _____.

In response to the _____, President John F. Kennedy sent a civil _____ bill to Congress. In 1964 Congress finally passed the Civil _____ Act. This act was important because, for the first time, there was a law to _____ voting _____, to provide access to public accommodations, to desegregate public facilities and public _____, and to provide equal employment opportunities. This same year, Martin Luther King, Jr., became the youngest _____ of the Nobel _____ _____.

Then, on April 4, 1968, while in Memphis, Tennessee, to _____ a strike by black workers, King was _____. Many thousands of people —black and white— mourned his _____. The United States, and indeed the world, had lost a symbol of hope.

King's dream was that one day:

. . . all of God's children, black men and white men, Jews and Gentiles, Protestants and Catholics, will be able to join hands and sing in the words of the old Negro _____ "_____ at last! _____ at last! Thank God Almighty, we are _____ at last."

*Alfred Nobel*

*The front of the prizes for Physiology and Medicine, Physics and Chemistry, and Literature*

# *Listening Exercise 7*

## Lech

# Walesa

*(Reading on page 15)*

## *Key Words*

| *New* | *Old* |
|-------|-------|
| growth | peace |
| released | free |
| genius | elect |
| activities, active | lead |
| formed, reform | politics |
| opposition | born |
| achieve | die |
| solve, solution | oppress |
| accept | lead |
| allowed | nonviolence |
| understanding | receive |
| serious | elect |
| fellow | arrest |
| policies | movement |
| | goal |
| | award |
| | prize |
| | support |
| | recognize |

# Lech Walesa

In Poland in 1989, for the first time in history, a communist government was _____ defeated in _____ _____. This remarkable event was the result of the slow and steady _____ of Solidarity, a trade union. Under the _____ of Lech Walesa, Solidarity slowly developed throughout the 70's and 80's into a powerful _____ force. Poland—Solidarity—Walesa: these three words are inseparable.

Lech Walesa was _____ on September 29, 1943, in Popow, Poland. His father, Boleslaw Walesa, was a carpenter who _____ two months after he was _____ from doing hard labor in one of the Nazi work camps. Lech was only eighteen months old at the time. His mother, Feliksa Walesa, married her husband's brother, Stanislaw Walesa, a year later. There were seven children, and they all worked on the family's small farm. Their home was small and without electricity. And so, this was the humble beginning of a man who inspired his country towards _____ from the _____ rule of Communism. Lech Walesa has been called "a _____ _____, an instinctive _____ who knows what the crowd is thinking before the crowd knows it, an apostle of _____ in the tradition of Gandhi and Martin Luther King."

After Walesa _____ his training at a vocational school in Lipno, Poland, he started working as an electrician at a shipyard in the Baltic port of Gdansk, Poland. By 1976 he was labeled a troublemaker because of his _____ with the workers union at the shipyard. He was fired from his job. His work with the union, however, continued. Then in 1980, the Solidarity movement was _____ as the first independent trade union in a Soviet-controlled country. In September, 1981, Walesa was _____ president of Solidarity and called for many economic and social _____.

By December 1981, the Communist government imposed martial law, and _____ of the trade unions, _____ groups, intellectuals, and some clergy were _____. Walesa was taken to a cabin in the wilderness where he stayed for eleven months under the guard of the government. After he was _____ in November 1982, he was watched and followed closely. The Solidarity _____ was outlawed but remained _____, and Walesa secretly met with the Temporary Coordinating Committee of Solidarity. Throughout its history, Solidarity has used _____ means to _____ its _____, and in 1983 Walesa was _____ the Nobel _____ _____ for his "determination to _____ his country's problems through negotiation and cooperation without resorting to _____."

Walesa did not travel to Oslo, Norway, to _____ the _____ because he feared that he would not be _____ back into Poland. His wife, Daunta, went in his place and delivered his speech. That night, outside their apartment window, a crowd of _____ gathered, and Lech Walesa said:

I see this as a _____ for us all, as a reward to each of us who wished to attain the truth by following the course of _____ and common _____. I believe that if foreigners can _____ us . . . then sooner or later we will be _____ by authorities in our

79

own country. I still believe the day will come when we will sit down together at the same table and come to an _____ about what is best for Poland, because whether we like it or not, we have no choice but to come to an _____; there is no other _____. I hope that the Nobel _____ will help us _____ this _____.

The political and economic problems facing Poland's new non-communist government in 1989 were very _____. Tadeusz Mazoviechi, the new prime minister, was an old friend of Walesa's and a _____ Solidarity member. Walesa, however, disagreed with many of the _____ of the new government and of the president, who was a communist. In 1990 the constitution was revised giving the president more power. Walesa ran for the presidency and won becoming the first noncommunist president of modern Poland.

*Listening Exercise 8*

Albert

# Schweitzer

*(Reading on page 18)*

## Key Words:
### New

philosophy
medicine, medical
fortunate
author
help, helpfully
treat
building, built, rebuild
remained
declare

### Old

theology
humanitarianism
service
born
excel
right
establish
enter
mission
suffer
grow
award
peace
prize
cause
die
devote

# Albert Schweitzer

Albert Schweitzer was a doctor of _____, _____, music, and _____. His name is synonymous with _____ because he is known throughout the world for his _____ to _____ and reverence for all life—plant, animal, and _____.

He was _____ on January 14, 1875, in Kayersburg, Alsace, which was part of Germany and later part of France after World War I. He was a sensitive young boy—sensitive to nature, to music, and to the feelings of those around him. He _____ in his academic studies and in music. At the age of twenty-one, young Schweitzer began to question his _____ to have such a _____ life without doing something in return for those less _____. He made a secret promise to himself that he would continue studying and living for himself until he was thirty; then for the rest of his life he would be of direct _____ to _____.

Schweitzer followed in his father's footsteps and was a minister. By the age of thirty he had also _____ himself as an _____, a lecturer, and a musician. He desired to preach the gospel of love through work as well as words, to use his hands as well as his mind. It was at this time that he learned of the great need of _____ doctors in the Congo region of Africa. He decided to become a doctor of _____, and even though his family and friends were surprised and upset about his decision, he _____ _____ school at the University of Strasbourg, Germany.

_____ school took six years. After Schweitzer passed his _____ exams, he completed a year of internship at a hospital and took a course in tropical _____. He was thirty-seven when he was finally prepared to begin his life of _____ to the sick in the African Congo. Before he left for Africa, Schweitzer married Helen Bresslau, a university professor's daughter who had taken a nursing course so that she could _____ her future husband in Africa.

On Easter Day, 1913, Dr. and Mrs. Schweitzer sailed for West Africa with boxes of equipment and _____ donated by friends who wanted to help _____ a hospital at the Lambaréné _____ in Africa. The morning after the Schweitzers arrived, patients _____ from sleeping sickness, malaria, heart trouble, dysentery, leprosy, injuries, and accidents came to be _____. The Schweitzers _____ their patients from an old henhouse, but it was not long before a new hospital _____ was _____ with the _____ and the trust of the African people.

Their work was interrupted by World War I. The Schweitzers, being German citizens in a French colony in Africa, were sent to a prison camp in France. In 1924 Dr. Schweitzer was finally able to return to Lambaréné to _____ the hospital. Mrs. Schweitzer _____ behind in Europe with their young daughter, Rhenna.

When Mrs. Schweitzer returned to Africa in 1929, the hospital at Lambaréné had _____ extensively, and there was a well-equipped operating room and a _____ staff of doctors and nurses. It was very different from the beginning days when Dr. and Mrs. Schweitzer _____ patients in the henhouse.

In 1953 Dr. Schweitzer was _____ the Nobel _____ _____. He was grateful but said, "No man has the _____ to pretend that he has worked enough for the _____ of _____ or _____ himself satisfied."

On the morning of September 4, 1965, in his ninetieth year, Dr. Schweitzer _____. He was buried next to his wife in a simple grave at Lambaréné.

Dr. Albert Schweitzer chose to live by a _____ that he called "the reverence for life." In one of his books, *Out of My Life and Thought*, he wrote:

> A man is ethical only when life, as such, is sacred to him, that of plants and animals as were as that of his fellow men, and when he _____ himself _____ to all life that is in need of _____.

*Listening Exercise 9*

Andrei D.

# Sakharov

*(Reading on page 21)*

## Key Words:
### New

research
science, scientist,
   scientific
speak out/spoke out
criticized
catastrophe
reality
champion
rehabilitated
leading
publicly
officially

### Old

| | |
|---|---|
| human | receive |
| right | peace |
| activist | prize |
| born | prevent |
| graduate | accept |
| weapon | arrest |
| contribute | exile |
| award | tragic, tragedy |
| elect | |
| member | |
| honor | |
| lead | |
| educate | |
| free | |
| help | |
| establish | |
| treat | |
| express | |
| punish | |
| allow | |
| message | |
| recognize | |

# Andrei D. Sakharov

Andrei Sakharov was a Soviet physicist and _____ _____ _____. He was _____ in Moscow on May 21, 1921.

In 1942 Sakharov _____ from Moscow University and later from the Lebedev Institute of Physics in 1947 with a Ph.D. in physics. During World War II, he was an engineer in a war plant, and from 1948 until 1956, he worked in _____ _____. He was an important _____ to the Soviet Union's development of nuclear _____ and is often referred to as "the father of the hydrogen bomb." For his outstanding _____, the Soviet government _____ him three Orders of Socialist Labor, the Soviet Union's highest civilian _____. He was also _____ a full _____ to the Academy of _____ in 1953, another _____ in Sakharov's career as a _____.

The Soviet _____ were proud of Sakharov and his accomplishments because he was a Russian who was _____ only in Soviet schools and therefore an example of the best of the Soviet _____ system.

Then, only four years after the first test of the power and effects of the Soviet hydrogen bomb in 1953, Sakharov began to _____ _____ against nuclear _____. He had realized the impact of radioactive contamination and the potential international danger of nuclear _____.

He became an embarrassment for the Soviet Union. How could "the father of the hydrogen bomb" now be _____ _____ against

nuclear _____? Sakharov also _____ his government's sup-

pression of _____ and the individual personality. He published his

first book, *Progress, Coexistence, and Intellectual* _____, in 1968.

In this book he pleaded for international cooperation to share the

benefits of _____ progress and to avoid a nuclear _____. He

warned the world about polluting the environment, and he _____

the Soviet government's position on _____ _____.

In 1970 Sakharov _____ to _____ the Moscow

_____ _____ Committee. He publicly _____ the

Soviet government's _____ of his colleagues and friends who had

been _____ and imprisoned for _____ opinions which were

different from those of the government. Sakharov and the Committee also

_____ _____ against the Soviet policy of denying a Soviet

citizen the _____ to emigrate to another country. The Soviet

government _____ Sakharov by not _____ him to continue

his _____ work.

Sakharov's voice was being heard, and the importance of his

_____ was _____ —if not in his own country, then around

the world. In 1974 he _____ the Eleanor Roosevelt _____

_____ and in 1975 he was _____ the Nobel _____

_____ for his work for _____ _____. The Soviet

government, however, _____ Sakharov from travelling to Oslo,

Norway, to _____ his _____. Then finally, in January of

1985, he was _____, his Soviet _____ were taken from him,

and he was _____ from Moscow to Gorky.

The Soviet government tried to silence Sakharov, but his _____ has reached around the world. He said:

The _____ of the contemporary world is complex with many planes. It is a fantastic mix of _____, irreparable misfortunes, apathy, prejudices, and ignorance, plus dynamism, selflessness, hope, and intelligence. The future may be even more _____. Or it may be more worthy of _____ beings—better and more intelligent. Or, again, it may not be at all. It depends on all of us . . . in every country of the world. It depends on our wisdom, our _____ from illusion and prejudices, our readiness to work, to practice intelligent austerity and on our kindness and our breadth as _____ beings.

So even if Sakharov's own country did not at that time _____ the value and intelligence of his _____ to the world, the Nobel _____ Committee _____ Sakharov as "one of the great _____ of _____ _____ in our age."

In 1988 and 1989 as the great changes occurred in the Soviet Union, Sakharov was _____. He returned from Gorky and spoke out in favor of the Gorbachev reforms. He was elected to the new, more democratic parliament where he was one of the _____ spokesmen for change and justice. He died suddenly on December 15, 1989, and was _____ and _____ mourned by the entire nation, led by President Gorbachev.

## *Listening Exercise 10*

### Naguib

# Mahfouz

*(Reading on page 24)*

## *Key Words:*
### *New*

literature, literate
writing, write, written
published
article
novel, novelist
famous
volume
threatened

### *Old*

born
birth
philosophy
enter
grow
author
receive
religion
research
recognize
award
prize
form
mankind
criticize

# Naguib Mahfouz

Naguib Mahfouz is to Arabic _____ what Mark Twain was to American _____, "an original with a deep feeling for his people." His _____, although deeply Egyptian and Arabic, has a universal appeal.

Naguib Mahfouz was _____ in 1911 in Cairo, Egypt (the exact date of his _____ is not known). He was the youngest of seven children. As a teenager he was an avid reader and moviegoer. He began _____ when he was seventeen and was a student of _____ and language in high school. In 1930 he _____ the University of Cairo. During this time, he _____ his first _____ and continued to enjoy _____ other _____ and short stories. His interest in _____ _____, and some of his favorite _____ were Tolstoy, Dostoevsky, Chekhov, and Proust. He _____ his B.A. degree in 1934 and was enrolled in a master's degree program in _____, but he chose instead to pursue his love of _____ and dropped out of the program. He _____ his first collection of short stories in 1938, *A Whisper of Madness*.

In 1939, Mahfouz began working in the Ministry of _____ Affairs. He worked there for fifteen years and continued to _____. Some of his well-known _____ _____ during this time were: *Games of Fate, Khan al-Khalili,* and *New Cairo*. Then in 1956, *Between Two Palaces* was _____. This was the book that made Mahfouz

_____, and it became the most popular _____ in the Arabic language. It is about a Cairo family from the end of World War I to 1944. It has recently been _____ for the first time in English, and the new title is *Palace Walk*. It is the first _____ of a trilogy. The other two _____ are *The Palace of Desire* and *The Sugar Bowl*. The trilogy took eleven years to complete—one year for _____, six years to _____, and four years to put into print. Time is a constant theme in his _____. Mahfouz says that "the hero of *Palace Walk* is time . . . everything changes because of time."

For many years the Arab world has thought of Naguib Mahfouz as its greatest living _____. In 1988 Mahfouz was internationally _____ when he was _____ the Nobel _____ in _____.

The Nobel Committee stated that he "has _____ an Arabic narrative art that applies to all _____."

When Mahfouz was asked about the importance of the Nobel _____ to Egypt and the Arab world, he replied:

It's given me for the first time in my life the feeling that my _____ could be on the international level. Egypt and the Arab world also get the Nobel _____ with me. I believe that from now on the international doors have opened and in the future, _____ people will look for Arab _____, and Arab _____ deserves that _____.

Mahfouz has _____ over thirty _____. Those _____ in English include: *Palace Walk, Wedding Song, The Thief and the Dogs,* and *The Beginning and the End.* Some of his work has been _____ by Muslim fundamentalists, and his life has been _____ by them. Nevertheless, he continues to _____ and live in Agouza, a suburb of Cairo, with his wife and two daughters.

Bertrand

# Russell

*(Reading on page 27)*

## *Key Words:*
## *New*                    ## *Old*

| | | |
|---|---|---|
| considered | influence | literature |
| social, socialism | philosophy | recognize |
| autobiography | write | champion |
| impress | born | human |
| logic, logician | die | free |
| controversial | politics | search |
| pacifism, pacifistic | spirit | suffer |
| respected | excel | mankind |
| fiction | remain | |
| | volume | |
| | establish | |
| | found | |
| | cause | |
| | oppose | |
| | involve | |
| | activity | |
| | declare | |
| | catastrophe | |
| | science | |
| | remain | |
| | award | |
| | prize | |

# Bertrand Russell

Bertrand Russell is _____ to be one of the most _____ _____ thinkers and _____ of the 20th century.

He was _____ on May 18, 1872, in Trelleck, Wales. His parents _____ when he was very young, and he lived with his paternal grandparents at Pembroke Lodge in Richmond Park, Surrey, England. His grandfather was Prime Minister of Great Britain twice, but it was his grandmother who was the most important _____ on his _____ and _____ conscience. In his _____, Russell _____:

Her fearlessness, her public _____, her contempt for convention, and her indifference to the opinion of the majority have always seemed good to me and have _____ themselves upon me as worthy of imitation.

He was tutored at home until he was almost sixteen. He was an _____ student and _____ in mathematics. From 1890 until 1894, he attended Trinity College, Cambridge University, and _____ there as a fellow from 1895 to 1901 and then as a lecturer from 1910 to 1916.

While at Cambridge, he collaborated with Alfred North Whithead (a Cambridge professor) on what was to become one of Russell's most important works, *Principia Mathematica*. It consists of three _____ and was _____ from 1910 through 1913. The basis of the work shows that the concepts of mathematics may be defined with the vocabulary of__ _____. *Principia Mathematica* _____ Bertrand Russell as one of the _____ fathers of modern analytical _____. Both _____ and _____ of mathematics considered it to be the most important work on _____ in the 20th century.

Russell was, however, dismissed from Cambridge because of his association with _____ _____ such as _____, _____ to Britain's _____ in World War I, and _____. In 1918 the British government imprisoned him for his _____ _____.

He continued to be _____ _____ and _____ throughout his ninety-seven years. In 1955, Bertrand Russell and Albert Einstein _____ the Russell-Einstein Manifesto—a public _____ to people and governments of the world about the necessity of avoiding war and potential nuclear _____. A week before Einstein _____, the Manifesto was signed by Russell, Einstein, and eight other world-renowned _____ including Frédéric Joliot-Curie. In 1958, Russell _____ the Campaign for Nuclear Disarmament. During the Cuban Missile Crisis, in 1962, he sent letters to U.S. President John F. Kennedy and Soviet Premier Nikita S. Khruschev pleading with them to meet and discuss disarmament. He protested the U.S. military _____ in Vietnam and, with French _____/ _____ Jean Paul Sartre, organized the Vietnam War Crimes Tribunal in Stockholm, Sweden.

Through the turbulent years of his life, Bertrand Russell _____ a prolific and well- _____ _____ in many fields, including _____, mathematics, _____ _____, _____, and even short works of _____. In 1950 he was _____ the Nobel _____ for _____ "in _____ of his varied and significant _____, in which he _____ _____ ideals and _____ of thought." Looking back on his life, he _____:

Three passions, simple but overwhelmingly strong, have governed my life: the longing for love, the _____ for knowledge and unbearable pity for the _____ of _____ . . . this has been my life. I have found it worth living, and would gladly live it again if the chance were offered me."

Gabriel José

# Garciá Márquez

*(Reading on page 30)*

## *Key Words:*
### *New*

fantasy, fantastic
raise
happenings, happening,
   happened
imagination, imaginative
developed
success
translated
style
conflict

### *Old*

| | |
|---|---|
| novel | critic |
| write | article |
| real, surreal | famous |
| message | publish |
| declare | remain |
| poor | struggle |
| grow up/grew up | fiction |
| born | logic |
| impress | death |
| graduate | peace |
| violence | prize |
| die | award |
| influence | literature |

# Gabriel José Garciá Márquez

Gabriel Garciá Márquez is an outstanding Colombian _____ and short-story _____. He is an extraordinary storyteller who combines _____ and _____. He says that the most important figure in his life was his grandfather, a retired army officer who told many long tales about his war days.

Today, Garciá Márquez carries on the fine tradition of story-telling and says that he is not concerned with morals or _____ in his stories—only in reporting the behavior of his characters. He says, "The _____ is not here to make _____ but to tell about things."

His own parents were too _ _____ to _____ Gabriel, so he _____ _____ in the large, gloomy house of his maternal grandparents. He was the oldest of twelve children and was _____ on March 6, 1928 in the village of Aracataca near the northern Caribbean coast of Colombia. His grandmother, who was interested in ghosts, spirits, and dead ancestors, loved to tell stories about strange and supernatural _____. It is clear in the _____ of Garciá Márquez that his grandparents made a big _____ on him and encouraged his _____.

When Gabriel was eight years old, he left his grandparents' house to go to school at the National Secondary School of Zipaquirá, near the capital of Colombia, Bogotá. After he _____ in 1946, he studied law at the University of Bogotá. He studied law for five years but never really liked it, so he never finished his degree.

Starting in 1948, there was a period of _____ in Colombia which lasted on and off for about ten years. Two hundred thousand people _____. It was during this time that Garciá Márquez _____ his first three books about what was _____ in his country. Afterwards, he studied journalism and in 1950 began to _____ for the daily paper *El Heraldo* in the town of Barranqilla. He did not earn much money, but he _____ as a _____. He was _____ by the _____ of Faulkner, Hemingway, Woolf, Kafka, and Joyce.

In 1954 he returned to Bogotá to be a film _____ and reporter for the newspaper *El Espectador*. He _____ a series of _____ about what really _____ in the disaster of a Colombian naval ship. The dictator of Colombia, Gustavo Rojas Pinilla, was embarrassed and angry. The _____, however, made Garciá Márquez _____ and were later _____ as a book. The newspaper sent him on assignment to Rome and Paris, but while he was in Paris, the paper was shut down by the Colombian government. He _____ in Paris for several years and then moved to Caracas, Venezuela. He never stopped _____, even though making a living was a _____.

In 1959 he began working as a journalist for the official press agency of Fidel Castro's Cuba, first in Bogotá, Colombia, and later in New York City. After taking a trip through Faulkner country to New Orleans, Garciá Márquez left his job and moved to Mexico City, México. From 1961 to 1965 he did not _____ any _____; he worked as a screenwriter, editor, and copywriter. Then one day in 1965, he began to _____ his masterpiece.

*One Hundred Years of Solitude* was first _____ in 1967 in Buenos Aires, Argentina. It was a huge _____ and sold over one million copies in Spanish. It was then _____ into at least twenty different languages and sold in more than twenty-five countries. _____ say it is a modern masterpiece. In writing this book, Garciá Márquez perfected his unique _____ that is very different from his early work when he was a journalist. The _____ are rich, detailed, and _____. It is like reading a dream, and the dream has its own _____ and _____. It is because of this that his _____ of _____ is described as _____, the definition of which is "having the intense irrational _____ of a dream." Garciá Márquez explains that "_____ comes from the _____ of Latin America."

The story of *One Hundred Years of Solitude* is about love and _____, war and _____, youth and age, in over six generations of the Buendiá family who live in the _____ town of Macondo where strange and supernatural things _____. Some say the story is really about the history of Latin America. The Nobel _____—winning Chilean poet, Pablo Neruda, says that the book is "perhaps the greatest revelation in the Spanish language since the *Don Quixote* of Cervantes."

In 1982 Gabriel Garciá Márquez was _____ the Nobel _____ in _____. The Nobel Committee said that he was _____ the _____, "for his _____ and short stories, in which the _____ and the _____ are combined in a richly composed world of _____, reflecting a continent's life and _____."

## *Listening Exercise 13*

## Pearl S.

# Buck

*(Reading on page 33)*

## *Key Words:*
## *New*                      *Old*

| | | |
|---|---|---|
| world | novel | literature |
| sympathetic, sympathy | human | receive |
| boundaries | famous | race |
| adapted | born | act |
| adopted, adoption | mission | death |
| insight | die | right |
| determination | grow up | develop |
| | raise | express |
| | teach | understand |
| | write | free |
| | autobiography | establish |
| | article | found |
| | conflict | contribution |
| | publish | respect |
| | real | social |
| | struggle | politics |
| | award | accept |
| | prize | threaten |
| | translate | |
| | exile | |

# Pearl S. Buck

Pearl S. Buck was an American _____, _____, and China's most _____, unofficial, Western interpreter.

She was _____ on June 26, 1892, in her mother's family home in the small town of Hillsboro, West Virginia. She was the fifth of seven children _____ to _____ parents Absalom and Caroline Sydenstricker. Three of the children _____ from tropical diseases, and Pearl _____ _____ as the eldest daughter.

When Pearl was five months old, her family sailed for China. She was _____ in the two _____ of East and West. Her beloved Chinese nurse, Wang Amah, cared for the young Pearl and was like her mother and _____ in the Chinese _____. Pearl _____ in her _____, *My Several* _____:

Thus I _____ _____ in a double _____, the small white clean Presbyterian American _____ of my parents and the big loving not-too-clean Chinese _____, and there was no communication between them. When I was in the Chinese _____, I was Chinese, I spoke Chinese and behaved as a Chinese ate as the Chinese did, and I shared their thoughts and feelings. When I was in the American _____, I shut the door between.

She began _____ in 1922, and in her many books, essays, _____, and short stories, Pearl Buck opened the door between these two _____. Throughout her _____ the _____ between East and West, old and new, are examined and explored.

Her first _____ _____ was *East Wind: West Wind (1930)*, a story about the contrasts between Eastern and Western civilizations. In 1931, her second and most well-known _____, *The Good Earth*, was _____. This was the _____ that changed Pearl Buck's life. The story was a _____, _____ portrayal of a Chinese peasant family—the hardships, the _____, the joys, and the sadness—the _____ that reached beyond the geographic and cultural _____. It was the first time the door of the mysterious Orient was opened wide and the Western _____ invited in. The book was _____ the Pulitzer _____ in 1932. It was on the best-seller list for months; it sold almost two million copies, was _____ into over thirty languages, was _____ for a Broadway play, and made into an _____—winning Hollywood film.

Pearl continued to _____ about China in *Sons* and *A House Divided*. She later _____ two _____ of her parents *The _____* and *Fighting Angel*. It was for these early works that she was _____ the 1938 Nobel _____ in _____. It was the first time an American woman had _____ a Nobel _____ in

_____. The Swedish Academy said during the _____ ceremony:

By _____ this year's _____ to Pearl Buck for the notable works which pave the way to a _____ _____ passing over widely separated _____ _____ and for the studies of _____ ideals . . . the Swedish Academy feels that it _____ in harmony and accord with the aim of Alfred Nobel's dreams for the future.

Pearl Buck continued to _____ until the time of her _____ on March 6, 1973 in Danby, Vermont. The variety of themes included: the _____ between work and marriage, women's _____, _____, _____marriage, _____ of the atomic bomb, her experiences as a mother of a retarded daughter, and widowhood.

She was a very productive _____, and by the end of her eighty-one years she had _____ over one hundred books, as well as countless speeches, _____, and scripts.

Her _____, however, was not the only way that she _____ her concerns for global _____ and _____ for all people. In her personal life she was the mother of ten children, only one of whom was her natural daughter. The other nine were her _____ children of different nationalities. In 1949 she _____

Welcome House, which was an _____ agency for Asian Americans.

Later, in 1964, she _____ the Pearl S. Buck _____ to assist

fatherless, and often stateless, half-American children throughout Asia.

Pearl Buck's _____ and _____ _____ made

her a _____ _____figure. Her _____ about China

are still very appropriate today in the face of China's _____ and

_____ turmoil. She said in 1938 in her Nobel Prize _____

speech:

The minds of my own country and of China, my foster country, are

alike in many ways, but above all, alike in our common love of

_____. And today more than ever, this is true, now when Chi-

na's whole being is engaged in the greatest of all _____, the

_____ for _____. I have never admired China more

than I do now when I see her uniting as she has never before, against

the enemy who _____ her _____. With this _____

for _____, which is in so profound a sense the essential quality

in her nature, I know she is unconquerable.

### Economics

*Crossed horns of plenty appear*
*beneath a likeness of Alfred Nobel.*
*The North Star emblem of the Royal*
*Swedish Academy of Sciences*
*appears on the back of the medal.*

106

## *Listening Exercise 14*

## Paul A.

# Samuelson

*(Reading on page 37)*

## *Key Words:*

### *New*

economics, economic,
   economist
level
theory
public
policy
improvement
standard
consumption, consume
puzzle

### *Old*

born
educate
receive
write
found
world
consider
success
influence
publish
award
prize
science
respect
accept
determine
real
social
solve
service
human
insight

# Paul Anthony Samuelson

Paul Samuelson was _____ on May 15, 1915, in Gary, Indiana. He was _____ at the University of Chicago in Illinois, where he _____ his B.S. degree in 1935. He continued his studies at Harvard University in Massachusetts and _____ M.A. in 1936 and his Ph.D. in 1941. He is Institute Professor of _____ at the Massachusetts Institute of Technology.

In 1947 Samuelson _____ _____ of _____ *Analysis* in which he used the language of mathematics to explain the _____ of _____. In 1948 he _____ _____ which is _____ to be the most _____ and _____ _____ text of our time. _____ is still being _____ in new, revised editions today.

Samuelson was _____ the 1970 Nobel _____ in _____ for doing "more than any other contemporary _____ to raise the _____ of _____ analysis in _____ _____."

In addition, Samuelson _____ a regular column for *Newsweek* magazine and is _____ to be one of the _____ most _____ _____. He is unlike many _____ because he

"_____ the fact that in a democracy, _____ choice, rather than _____ or ideology, will _____ _____ _____."

He _____ himself to be a liberal and, therefore, concerned with _____ in living _____ and reductions in inequality. He says:

My own concern is with _____ in living _____, not with expansion in bureaucrats' power. Reductions in inequality of condition and opportunity matter more than fulfillment of five-year plans or _____ of programs for _____ reconstruction.

In _____ there are three languages that may be used. Samuelson insists that mathematics is a language and prefers using it to explain and _____ _____ problems. An example using the three different languages to explain the same thing follows:

### Mathematics

$$c = f(y)$$

c = consumption          y = income          f = function

### Economese

consumption function

or

propensity-to-consume schedule

### English

The more we earn, the more we spend; but as our incomes rise,

we increase our spending less and less and increase

our saving more and more.

Samuelson, who has six children, says:

> I think having children is the biggest kick in life . . . but aside from that, the greatest pleasure I have—the greatest personal pleasure—is in the _____ - _____ aspect of _____, the mathematical work. But in the end, the _____ is a much better _____ if it isn't just a _____, if it has relevance to _____ -_____ problems.

Samuelson's life work has been to use _____ in the _____ of _____. He is a pioneer in the "reconstruction of _____ into a coherent and orderly discipline. He has done more than anyone of his time to disseminate its _____ and to _____ government _____ at the highest _____."

*Listening Exercise 15*

Milton

# Friedman

*(Reading on page 40)*

## Key Words:
### New

capitalism,
   capitalistic
money, monetarism,
   monetary
contemporary
role
variety

### Old

| | |
|---|---|
| born | standard |
| educate | world |
| receive | award |
| consider | prize |
| economy | influence |
| champion | research |
| free | theory |
| famous | |
| policy | |
| level | |
| activity | |
| politics | |
| improve | |
| advocate | |
| protect | |
| science | |
| literature | |
| human | |
| understand | |
| achieve | |
| genius | |
| social | |

# Milton Friedman

Milton Friedman was _____ on July 31, 1912 in Brooklyn, New York. He was _____ at Rutgers University in New Jersey and _____ his B.A. degree in 1932. He attended the University of Chicago in Illinois and _____ his M.A. degree in 1933. In 1946, he _____ his Ph.D. from Columbia University in New York.

He is _____ to be America's best-known conservative _____. He is a _____ of the _____-market and one of the most effective defenders of _____ in America. Friedman is most _____ for his work on _____ and a new kind of _____ that he introduced called "_____." _____ challenged the thinking of most _____, including Paul A. Samuelson, Friedman's _____. Simply stated, Friedman believes that the role of _____ _____ (the regulation by the Federal Reserve System of the nation's _____ supply and interest rates) plays a bigger part than previously thought in the _____ of _____ _____ and the price _____.

In his book _____ *and* _____(1962), Friedman discusses the role of competitive _____ "the organization of the bulk of _____ _____ through private enterprise operating in a _____ market—as a system of _____ _____ and a necessary condition for _____ _____." He further states that he believes that the government's _____ in the _____ enterprise system should be very limited—a belief that makes him popular with industry and businessmen and different from leading _____ _____ who look for ways to use government to _____ the performance of the _____ and to advance _____ welfare. He further _____ a decentralization of governmental power:

> The preservation of _____ is the _____ reason for limit-
> ing and decentralizing governmental power. But there is also a
> constructive reason. The great advances of civilization, whether in
> architecture or painting, in _____ or _____, in industry
> or agriculture, have never come from centralized government. . . .
> Newton and Leibnitz; Einstein and Bohr; Shakespeare, Milton, and
> Pasternak; Whitney, McCormick, Edison, and Ford; Jane Addams,
> Florence Nightingale, and Albert Schweitzer; no one of these opened
> new frontiers in _____ knowledge and _____, in
> _____, in technical possibilities, or in the relief of
> _____ misery in response to governmental directives. Their
> _____ were the product of individual _____, of
> strongly held minority views, of a _____ climate permitting
> _____ and diversity.
>
> Government can never duplicate the _____ and diversity of
> individual action. At any moment in time, by imposing uniform
> _____ in housing, or nutrition, or clothing, government could
> undoubtedly _____ the _____ of living of many indi-
> viduals. . . . But in the process, government would replace progress by
> stagnation, it would substitute uniform mediocrity for the
> _____ essential for that experimentation. . . ."

Friedman says that _____ is a prerequisite for _____ _____, that the combination of _____ and _____ brings a hope of a better _____. _____ does not, however, guarantee a _____ state. In fact, there are many countries in the world today with _____ _____ where civil liberties are denied daily. Friedman admits that it is possible for a country to be _____ _____ and yet not _____ _____.

In 1976, Milton Friedman was _____ the Nobel _____ in _____, and the Nobel Committee noted his book _____ *and* _____ and added that it is "very rare for an _____ to wield such _____, directly or indirectly, not only on the direction of _____ _____ but also on the actual practice." His _____ have _____ _____ and _____ makers in the United States and the _____.

# Michael Stuart Brown
and
# Joseph Leonard Goldstein

*(Reading on page 43)*

## Key Words:
### New

staff
health
genetic, genetics
disease
control
blood
collect
receptor
revolutionized

### Old

born
receive
medicine
research
role
science
understand
cause
world
level
raise
form
prize
award
treat

# Michael Stuart Brown and
# Joseph Leonard Goldstein

Michael Stuart Brown was _____ in New York City, New York, on April 13, 1941. He _____ both his B.A. and M.D. degrees from the University of Pennsylvania.

Joseph Leonard Goldstein was _____ on April 18, 1940, in Sumter, South Carolina. He _____ his B.S. degree in 1962 from Washington and Lee University in Lexington, Virginia. Then, in 1966, he _____ his M.D. degree from Southwestern _____ School, University of Texas in Dallas.

Dr. Brown and Dr. Goldstein met in 1966 when they were both interns and later residents at Massachusetts General Hospital in Boston. They became close friends. In 1968, after residency, they both joined the _____ of the National Institute of _____ in Bethesda, Maryland, to gain experience in _____. Dr. Goldstein's _____ focused on the _____ aspects of heart _____. Dr. Brown's _____ was primarily on the _____ of enzymes in the chemistry of the digestive system. In 1971, Dr. Brown continued his _____ as a _____ fellow at the University of Texas _____ _____ Center in Dallas. It was here that he began studying the _____ of an enzyme that _____ cholesterol production. A year later, Dr. Goldstein joined the Center as head of the _____ school's first department of _____ _____.

The focus of his work was to try to _____ _____ the basic defect in the

_____ _____, FHC or familial hypercholesterolemia. FHC

was first identified as a _____ _____ in 1939, by Carl Müller

of Oslo, Norway. Müller found that a _____ defect _____

the condition which resulted in high blood cholesterol _____ and

heart attacks, sometimes in very young people. And so, Dr. Brown and Dr.

Goldstein worked together to try to _____ the cholesterol

problem.

To _____ the importance of their _____ it is necessary to

know some facts about cholesterol. There are two sources of cholesterol,

the body's liver and fat in food. Cholesterol is essential to the life of cells,

which take in cholesterol from the _____. Lipoproteins carry

cholesterol throughout the _____-stream. There are low-density

lipoproteins (L.D.L.) and high-density lipoproteins (H.D.L.). L.D.L. cho-

lesterol is "bad" and may be the _____ of _____ problems.

H.D.L. is the "good" cholesterol because it takes the L.D.L. away from the

linings of the arteries where it likes to _____, clogging the arteries

and _____ heart disease. Coronary heart _____ kills more

people in the Western _____ than any other _____, and

atherosclerosis, hardening of the arteries, kills one million Americans

each year.

So, what Dr. Brown and Dr. Goldstein found was that cells make L.D.L.

_____ that take in cholesterol from the _____ and that

people with FHC don't have enough L.D.L. _____. Dr. Goldstein

said, "Our work has pointed to the importance of this _____ in

_____ of _____ cholesterol and how the _____

can be _____ through drugs and a low-cholesterol, low-fat diet." If a person eats food high in cholesterol, then more of the "bad" cholesterol flows through the _____ stream, more is available to the cells, fewer L.D.L. _____ _____ to absorb cholesterol, and so more cholesterol _____ on the arterial walls and blocks _____ to the heart.

The 1985 Nobel _____ in Physiology or _____ was _____ to Dr. Brown and Dr. Goldstein. The Nobel Committee stated that their _____ has "_____ our knowledge about the regulation of cholesterol metabolism and the _____ of _____ _____ by abnormally elevated cholesterol _____ in the _____."

*Listening Exercise 17*

Albert

# Einstein

*(Reading on page 46)*

## *Key Words:*
### *New*

physicist, physics
    physical
profession, professor
matter
institute
citizenship, citizen
energy

### *Old*

| | |
|---|---|
| theory | form |
| world | revolutionize |
| contribution | accept |
| science | remain |
| philosophy | death |
| pacifism | establish |
| born | write |
| success | catastrophe |
| enter | understand |
| graduate | contemporary |
| teach | controversy |
| politics | spirit |
| religion | violence |
| free | oppose |
| develop | express |
| genius | courage, |
| recognize |     courageously |
| member | |
| award | |
| prize | |
| social | |
| research | |

# Albert Einstein

It is generally thought that Albert Einstein was the greatest _____ _____ who has ever lived. His ideas and _____ changed the _____. Some of his major _____ in _____ were the _____ of relativity ($E=mc^2$), quantum _____, and statistical _____. He was also a _____ _____ and _____.

Albert Einstein was _____ on March 14, 1879, in Ulm, Germany. His interest in _____ began when he was only five years old. His father had given him a magnetic compass, and the young Albert wondered about the unseen forces that made the compass needle point north.

In school, Albert was not a very good student. When his father went to speak with the schoolmaster about what _____ his son should choose, the schoolmaster replied that it did not _____ because Albert Einstein would never make a _____ of anything. Albert dropped out of school at fifteen because he hated strick discipline and rote learning. He loved playing the violin and mathematics.

When his family moved to Milan, Italy, Albert decided he wanted to study _____ at the Swiss Federal _____ of Technology in Zürich, Switzerland. His father tried to convince him to forget this "_____ nonsense" and take up the "sensible trade" of electrical engineering. Albert, however, had other plans.

He failed the Institute's _____ exam, but after a year's study at a school near Zürich he passed and _____ in 1896. He _____ in 1900. He was unable to get a university _____ position so he became a private _____ and mathematics tutor for two years. During this time, he renounced his German _____ and became a Swiss _____ on February 21, 1901. He maintained his Swiss _____ throughout his life. He was proud of it because he thought Switzerland was a country of cultural diversity, _____ and _____ tolerance, and personal _____.

In 1902 Einstein took a job in the Swiss Patent Office in Bern. The work was not very demanding so he had plenty of time to _____ his _____ that would later change _____ forever. He married Mileva Maric (a former classmate at the _____) in 1903, and they had two sons, Hans Albert and Edward. In 1909, at the age of thirty, Einstein finally left his job at the Patent Office and began his life-long career in the academic _____. His _____ had begun to be _____, and by 1914 he was at the top of his _____ as a _____ of the Royal Prussian Academy of _____ in Berlin. In 1921 he was _____ the Nobel _____ in _____. Because Einstein's _____ were shaking the scientific world and _____, their validity was often challenged, _____, and debated by others. He was _____ the Nobel _____ for his _____ of the photoelectric effect and not for his better-known _____ of Relativity (E=mc²) because too few _____ could fully comprehend it. Simply stated, it means that (m) _____ and (e) energy are the same things only in different _____. This idea, however, _____ the _____ perception of the _____ universe.

In 1933, when Adolf Hitler came into power, Einstein and his second wife, his cousin Elsa, moved to Princeton, New Jersey. He became a _____ at the _____ for Advanced Study where he _____ until his _____ on April 18, 1955. During these latter years he became interested in Zionism—the preservation of Jewish heritage and the _____ of a Jewish homeland. He was a _____, and shortly before his _____ he _____ and signed the Russell-Einstein Manifesto which warned the people and governments of the _____ about the potential of nuclear _____.

Albert Einstein is remembered as the greatest _____ in the _____, the absent-minded _____, a Zionist, a _____, and a wise man. Einstein was often _____ by his _____, but this is often the case with _____—it is not fully _____ in the time that it appears. Einstein could have been _____ about himself when he _____ this about his friend the _____ British _____ and _____, Bertrand Russell:

Great _____ have always encountered _____ _____ from mediocre minds. The mediocre mind is incapable of _____ the man who refuses to bow blindly to conventional prejudices and chooses instead to _____ his opinions _____ and honestly.

# Irène Joliot-Curie
and
# Frédéric Joliot

*(Reading on page 49)*

## Key Words:
### New

radioactive, radiation
discovered, discovery
chemistry
laboratory
benefitting, beneficial
   benefitted

### Old

| | |
|---|---|
| born | write |
| famous | weapon |
| dedicate | threaten |
| science | mankind |
| research | real |
| award | public |
| prize | peace |
| physics | social |
| die | solve |
| grow up | develop |
| world | human |
| graduate | profession |
| institute | cause |
| staff | devote |
| educate | death |
| money | treat |
| excellent | disease |
| raise | |
| honor | |
| blood | |
| energy | |
| matter | |

# Irène and Frédéric Joliot-Curie

Irène Joliot-Curie was _____ on September 12, 1897, in Paris, France. Her _____ parents, Marie and Pierre Curie, had _____ their lives to the _____ _____ of _____ elements. The Curies had _____ two _____ elements: polonium and radium. In 1903 they were jointly _____ the Nobel _____ in _____ for the _____ of radium. Pierre Curie _____ in 1906, but Marie Curie continued their work, and in 1911 she was _____ the Nobel _____ again, this time in _____, for isolating the element of radium. Marie Curie was the first woman to be _____ a Nobel _____ in _____ or _____ and her daughter, Irène, became the second.

Irène _____ _____ in the _____ of _____. After she graduated from the University of Paris, she began to work at her parent's laboratory, the Curie _____ of Radium, in Paris. She met Frédéric Joliot when he came to work on the _____ of _____.

Frédéric Joliot was _____ on March 19, 1900, in Paris, France. He was well-_____ even though his parents did not have a lot of _____. He also _____ from the University of Paris and in 1925 began working at the Curie _____. A year later, Irène and Frédéric were married, on October 4, 1926.

They decided to hyphenate their last names to symbolize that they worked together in an equal partnership and to carry on the Curie name.

Irène was shy and serious; Frédéric was gregarious and loved to talk. They complemented each other and made an _____ team. Together they _____ their children, Hélène and Pierre, and together they worked many long hours in the _____.

Their _____ of _____ artificial isotopes earned them the 1935 Nobel _____ in _____. Marie Curie _____ only a few weeks before this _____ was _____ to her daughter. Marie Curie _____ of a condition in which the bone marrow fails to make the necessary red _____ cells. It was _____ by the years of exposure to _____ in the _____.

Irène and Frédéric had been working on changing stable elements into _____ ones, and for the first time a way had been found to release by artificial means some of the _____ that Albert Einstein had shown to exist in every atom of _____.

The Curies and the Joliot-Curies were good friends with Albert Einstein. In 1955, when Einstein and Bertrand Russell _____ the Russell-Einstein Manifesto, Frédéric Joliot-Curie was among the nine other _____ _____ who signed it. The conclusion of the Manifesto states:

In view of the fact that in any future war nuclear _____ will certainly be employed, and that any such _____ _____ the continued existence of _____, we urge the governments of the _____ to _____, and to acknowledge _____, that their purposes cannot be furthered by a _____ war, and we urge them, consequently, to find _____ means for the settlement of all _____ of dispute between them.

The Joliot-Curies were very much aware of their _____ responsibility as _____. They belonged to the _____ Federation of Associations of _____ Workers, an organization _____ to utilizing _____ as a means of _____ problems and _____ _____. Frédéric stated, "French _____ does not want to have anything to do with atomic _____ other than for _____. All our efforts are being utilized in the _____ of this tremendous _____ for the advancement of _____." He said this when he was the High Commissioner of France's first Atomic _____ Commission.

After full and rewarding personal and _____ lives, Irène and Frédéric Joliot-Curie _____ within two years of each other. Irène _____ on March 17, 1956, of leukemia. Leukemia is a form of cancer which can be _____ by x-ray or _____ exposure. Frédéric _____ on August 14, 1958, of liver and intestinal problems, also due to _____ exposure.

It is sadly ironic that the _____ _____ that Marie Curie and the Joliot-Curies had _____ their lives to eventually _____ their _____. The Joliot-Curie _____ isotopes have been further _____ and are used today in many _____ ways, including the diagnosis and _____ of _____ such as leukemia, other types of cancer, and thyroid _____. Because of their _____ and sense of responsibility, _____ has _____.

126

# The Winners of
# The Alfred B. Nobel Prize
## *Peace*

1901 Henri Dunant *(Switzerland)*; Frederick Passy *(France)*
1902 Elie Ducommun *and* Albert Gobat *(Switzerland)*
1903 Sir William R. Cremer *(England)*
1904 Institute de Droit International *(Belgium)*
1905 Bertha von Suttner *(Austria)*
1906 Theodore Roosevelt *(U.S.)*
1907 Ernesto T. Moneta *(Italy)* and Louis Renault *(France)*
1908 Klas P. Arnoldson *(Sweden)* and Frederik Bajer *(Denmark)*
1909 Auguste M. F. Beernaert *(Belgium)* and Baron Paul H. B. B. d'Estournelles de Constant de Rebecque *(France)*
1910 Bureau International Permanent de la Paix *(Switzerland)*
1911 Tobias M. C. Asser *(Holland)* and Alfred H. Fried *(Austria)*
1912 Elihu Root *(U.S.)*
1913 Henri La Fontaine *(Belgium)*
1915 No award
1916 No award
1917 International Red Cross
1919 Woodrow Wilson *(U.S.)*
1920 Léon Bourgeois *(France)*
1921 Karl H. Branting *(Sweden)* and Christian L. Lange *(Norway)*
1922 Fridtjof Nansen *(Norway)*
1923 No award
1924 No award
1925 Sir Austen Chamberlain *(England)* and Charles G. Dawes *(U.S.)*
1926 Aristide Briand *(France)* and Gustav Stresemann *(Germany)*
1927 Ferdinand Buisson *(France)* and Ludwig Quidde *(Germany)*
1928 No award
1929 Frank B. Kellogg *(U.S.)*
1930 Lars O. J. Söderblom *(Sweden)*
1931 Jane Addams *and* Nicholas M. Butler *(U.S.)*
1932 No award
1933 Sir Norman Angell *(England)*
1934 Arthur Henderson *(England)*
1935 Karl von Ossietzky *(Germany)*
1936 Carlos de S. Lamas *(Argentina)*
1937 Lord Cecil of Chelwood *(England)*
1938 Office International Nansen pour les Réfugiés *(Switzerland)*
1939 No award
1944 International Red Cross
1945 Cordell Hull *(U.S.)*
1946 Emily G. Balch *and* John R. Mott *(U.S.)*
1947 American Friends Service Committee *(U.S.) and* British Society of Friends' Service Council *(England)*
1948 No award

1949 Lord John Boyd Orr *(Scotland)*
1950 Ralph J. Bunche *(U.S.)*
1951 Léon Jouhaux *(France)*
1952 Albert Schweitzer *(French Equatorial Africa)*
1953 George C. Marshall *(U.S.)*
1954 Office of U.N. High Commissioner for Refugees
1955 No award
1956 No award
1957 Lester B. Pearson *(Canada)*
1958 Rev. Dominique Georges Henri Pire *(Belgium)*
1959 Philip John Noel-Baker *(England)*
1960 Albert John Luthuli *(South Africa)*
1961 Dag Hammarskjöld *(Sweden)*
1962 Linus Pauling *(U.S.)*
1963 Intl. Comm. of Red Cross; League of Red Cross Societies *(both Geneva)*
1964 Rev. Dr. Martin Luther King, Jr. *(U.S.)*
1965 UNICEF *(United Nations Children's Fund)*
1966 No award
1967 No award
1968 René Cassin *(France)*
1969 International Labour Organization
1970 Norman E. Borlaug *(U.S)*
1971 Willy Brandt *(West Germany)*
1972 No award
1973 Henry A. Kissinger *(U.S.)*; Le Duc Tho *(North Vietnam)*
1974 Eisaku Sato *(Japan)*; Sean MacBride *(Ireland)*
1975 Andrei D. Sakharov *(U.S.S.R)*
1976 Mairead Corrigan *and* Betty Williams *(both Northern Ireland)*
1977 Amnesty International
1978 Menachem Begin *(Israel)* and Anwar el-Sadat *(Egypt)*
1979 Mother Teresa of Calcutta *(India)*
1980 Adolf Pérez Esquivel *(Argentina)*
1981 Office of the United Nations High Commissioner for Refugees
1982 Alva Myrdal *(Sweden)* and Alfonso Garcia Robles *(Mexico)*
1983 Lech Walesa *(Poland)*
1984 Bishop Desmont Tutu *(South Africa)*
1985 International Physicians for the Prevention of Nuclear War
1986 Elie Wiesel *(U.S.)*
1987 Oscar Arias Sánchez *(Costa Rica)*
1988 U.N. Peacekeeping Forces
1989 The Dalai Lama *(Tibet)*
1990 Mikhail Gorbachev (U.S.S.R.)

# *Literature*

1901 René F. A. Sully Prudhomme *(France)*
1902 Theodor Mommsen *(Germany)*
1903 Björnstjerne Bjornson *(Norway)*
1904 Frédéric Mistral *(France)* and José Echegaray *(Spain)*
1905 Henryk Sienkiewicz *(Poland)*
1906 Giosurè Carducci *(Italy)*
1907 Rudyard Kipling *(England)*
1908 Rudolf Eucken *(Germany)*
1909 Selma Lagerlöf *(Sweden)*
1910 Paul von Heyse (Germany)
1911 Maurice Maeterlinck *(Belgium)*
1912 Gerhart Hauptmann *(Germany)*
1913 Rabindranath Tagore *(India)*

1915 Romain Rolland *(France)*
1916 Verner von Heidenstam *(Sweden)*
1917 Karl Gjellerup and Henrik Pontoppidan *(both Denmark)*
1919 Carl Spitteler *(Switzerland)*
1920 Knut Hamsun *(Norway)*
1921 Anatole France *(France)*
1922 Jacinto Benavente *(Spain)*
1923 William B. Yeats *(Ireland)*
1924 Wladyslaw Reymont *(Poland)*
1925 George Bernard Shaw *(England)*
1926 Grazia Deledda *(Italy)*
1927 Henri Bergson *(France)*
1928 Sigrid Undset *(Norway)*

# *Economics*

# *Medicine*

**Physiology or Medicine, continued**

1905 Robert Koch *(Germany), for work on tuberculosis*
1906 Camillo Golgi *(Italy),* and Santiago Ramón y Cajal *(Spain), for work on structure of the nervous system*
1907 Charles L. A. Laveran *(France), for work with protozoa in the generation of disease*
1908 Paul Ehrlich *(Germany),* and Elie Metchnikoff *(U.S.S.R), for work on immunity*
1909 Theodor Kocher *(Switzerland), for work on the thyroid gland*
1910 Albrecht Kossel *(Germany), for achievements in the chemistry of the cell*
1911 Allvar Gullstrand *(Sweden), for work on the dioptrics of the eye*
1912 Alexis Carrel *(France), for work on vascular ligature and grafting of blood vessels and organs*
1913 Charles Richet *(France), for work on anaphylaxy*
1914 Robert Bárány *(Austria), for work on physiology and pathology of the vestibular system*
1915-1918 No award
1919 Jules Bordet *(Belgium), for discoveries in connection with immunity*
1920 August Krogh *(Denmark), for discovery of regulation of capilaries' motor mechanism*
1921 No award
1922 *In 1923, the 1922 prize was shared by* Archibald V. Hill *(England), for discovery relating to heat production in muscles; and* Otto Meyerhof *(Germany), for correlation between consumption of oxygen and production of lactic acid in muscles*
1923 Sir Frederick Banting *(Canada),* and John J. R. Macleod *(Scotland), for discovery of insulin*
1924 Willem Einthoven *(Netherlands), for discovery of the mechanism of the electrocardiogram*
1925 No award
1926 Johannes Fibiger *(Denmark), for discovery of the Spiroptera carcinoma*
1927 Julius Wagner-Jauregg *(Austria), for use of malaria inoculation in treatment of dementia paralytica*
1928 Charles Nicolle *(France), for work on typhus exanthematicus*
1929 Christiaan Eijkman *(Netherlands), for discovery of the antineuritic vitamins; and* Sir Frederick Hopkins *(England), for discovery of growth-promoting vitamins*
1930 Karl Landsteiner *(U.S.), for discovery of human blood groups*
1931 Otto H. Waburg *(Germany), for discovery of the character and mode of action of the respiratory ferment*
1932 Sir Charles Sherrington *(England)* and Edgar D. Adrian *(U.S.), for discoveries of the function of the neuron*
1933 Thomas H. Morgan *(U.S.), for discoveries on hereditary function of the chromosomes*
1934 George H. Whipple, George R. Minot, *and* William P. Murphy *(U.S), for discovery of liver therapy against anemias*
1935 Hans Spemann *(Germany), for discovery of the organizer-effect in embryonic development*
1936 Sir Henry Dale *(England),* and Otto Loewi *(Germany), for discoveries on chemical transmission of nerve impulses*
1937 Albert Szent-Györgyi von Nagyrapolt *(Hungary), for discoveries on biological combustion*
1938 Corneille Heymans *(Belgium), for determining importance of sinus and aorta mechanisms in the regulation of respiration*
1939 Gerhard Domagk *(Germany), for antibacterial effect of prontocilate*
1943 *Henrik Dam (Denmark)* and Edward A. Doisy *(U.S.), for analysis of Vitamin K*
1944 Joseph Erlanger *and* Herbert Spencer Gasser *(U.S.), for work on functions of the nerve threads*
1945 Sir Alexander Fleming, Ernst Boris Chain, *and* Sir Howard Florey *(England), for discovery of penicillin*
1946 Herman J. Muller *(U.S.), for hereditary effects of X-rays on genes*
1947 Carl F. *and* Gerty T. Cori *(U.S.), for work on animal starch metabolism;* Bernardo A. Houssay *(Argentina), for study of pituitary*
1948 Paul Mueller *(Switzerland), for discovery of insect-killing properties of DDT*
1949 Walter Rudolf Hess *(Switzerland), for research on brain control of body; and* Antonio Caetano de Abreu Freire Egas Moniz *(Portugal), for development of brain operation*

1950 Philip S. Hench, Edward C. Kendall *(both U.S.), and* Tadeus Reichstein *(Switzerland), for discoveries about hormones of adrenal cortex*
1951 Max Theiler *(South Africa), for development of anti-yellow-fever vaccine*
1952 Selman A. Waksman *(U.S.), for co-discovery of streptomycin*
1953 Fritz A. Lipmann *(Germany-England),* and Hans Adolph Krebs *(Germany-England), for studies of living cells*
1954 John F. Enders, Thomas H. Weller, *and* Frederick C. Robbins *(U.S.), for work with cultivation of polio virus*
1955 Hugo Theorell *(Sweden), for work on oxidation enzymes*
1956 Dickinson W. Richards, Jr., André F. Cournand *(both U.S.), and* Werner Forssman *(Germany), for new techniques in treating heart disease*
1957 Daniel Bovet *(Italy), for development of drugs to relieve allergies and relax muscles during surgery*
1958 Joshua Lederberg *(U.S.), for work with genetic mechanisms;* George W. Beadie *and* Edward L. Tatum *(U.S.), for discovering how genes transmit hereditary characteristics*
1959 Severo Ochoa *and* Arthur Kornberg *(U.S.), for discoveries related to compounds within chromosomes, which play a vital role in heredity*
1960 Sir Macfarlane Burnet *(Australia)* and Peter Brian Medawar *(England), for discovery of acquired immunological tolerance*
1961 Georg von Bekesy *(U.S.), for discoveries about physical mechanisms of stimulation within cochlea*
1962 James D. Watson *(U.S.),* Maurice H. F. Wilkins, *and* Francis H. C. Crick *(England), for determining structure of deoxyribonucleic acid (DNA)*
1963 Alan Lloyd Hodgkin, Andrew Fielding Huxley *(both England),* and Sir John Carew Eccles *(Australia), for research on nerve cells*
1964 Konrad E. Bloch *(U.S.)* and Feodor Lynen *(Germany), for research on mechanism and regulation of cholesterol and fatty acid metabolism*
1965 François Jacob, André Lwolff, *and* Jacques Monod *(France), for study of regulatory activities in body cells*
1966 Charles Brenton Huggins *(U.S.), for studies in hormone treatment of cancer of prostate;* Francis Peyton Rous *(U.S.) for discovery of tumor-producing viruses*
1967 Haldan K. Hartline, George Wald, *and* Ragnar Granit *(U.S.), for work on human eye*
1968 Robert W. Holley, Har Gobind Khorana, *and* Marshall W. Nirenberg *(U.S.), for studies of genetic code*
1969 Max Delbruck, Alfred D. Hershey, *and* Salvador E. Luria *(U.S.), for study of mechanism of virus infection in living cells*
1970 Julius Axelrod *(U.S.),* Ulf S. von Euler *(Sweden), and* Sir Bernard Katz *(England), for studies of how nerve impulses are transmitted within the body*
1971 Earl W. Sutherland, Jr. *(U.S.) for research on how hormones work*
1972 Gerald M. Edelman *(U.S.),* and Rodney R. Porter *(U.K.), for research on the chemical structure and nature of antibodies*
1973 Karl von Frisch *and* Konrad Lorenz *(Austria), and* Nikolaas Tinbergen *(Netherlands), for their studies of individual and social behavior patterns*
1974 George E. Palade *and* Christian de Duve *(both U.S.), and* Albert Claude *(Belgium), for contributions to understanding inner workings of living cells*
1975 David Baltimore, Howard M. Temin, *and* Renato Dulbecco *(all U.S.), for work in interaction between tumor viruses and genetic material of the cell*
1976 Baruch S. Blumberg *and* D. Carleton Gajdusek *(U.S.), for discoveries concerning new mechanisms for the origin and dissemination of infectious diseases*
1977 Rosalyn S. Yallow, Roger C. L. Guillemin, *and* Andrew V. Schally *(all U.S.), for research in role of hormones in chemistry of the body*
1978 Daniel Nathans *and* Hamilton Smith *(both U.S.), and* Werner Arber *(Switzerland), for discovery of restriction enzymes and their application to problems of molecular genetics*
1979 Allan McLeod Cormack *(U.S.),* and Godfrey Newbold Hounsfield *(England), for developing computed axial tomography (CAT scan) X-ray technique*

1980 Baruj Benacerraf *and* George D. Snell *(both U.S.) and* Jean Dausset *(France), for discoveries that explain how the structure of cells relates to organ transplants and diseases*

1981 Roger W. Sperry *and* David H. Hubel *(both U.S.) and* Torsten N. Wiesel *(Sweden), for studies vital to understanding the organization and functioning of the brain*

1982 Sune Bergstrom *and* Bengt Samuelsson *(Sweden) and* John R. Vane *(U.K.), for research in prostaglandins, a hormonelike substance involved in a wide range of illnesses*

1983 Barbara McClintock *(U.S.), for her discovery of mobile genes in the chromosomes of a plant that change the future generations of plants they produce*

1984 Cesar Milstein *(U.K./Argentina)* Georges J. F. Kohler *(West Germany), and* Niels K. Jerne *(U.K./Denmark), for their work in immunology*

1985 Michael S. Brown *and* Joseph L. Goldstein *(both U.S.), for their work which has drastically widened our understanding of the cholesterol metabolism and increased our possibilities to prevent and treat atherosclerosis and heart attacks*

1986 Rita Levi-Montalcini *(U.S./Italy) and* Stanley Cohen *(U.S.), for their contributions to the understanding of substances that influence cell growth*

1987 Susumu Tomegawa *(Japan), for his discoveries of how the body can suddenly marshal its immunological defenses against millions of different disease agents that it has never encountered before*

1988 Gertrude B. Elion *and* George H. Hitchings *(both U.S.), and* Sir James Black *(U.K), for their discoveries of "important principles for drug treatment"*

1989 J. Michael Bishop *and* Harold E. Varmus, *(both U.S.), for their discovery that normal genes can cause cancer when they malfunction through mutation or changes caused by chemical carcinogens*

1990 E. Donnal Thomas *(U.S.), for being the first doctor to transfer bone marrow from one person to another in 1956.* Joseph Murray *(U.S.), for being the first doctor to perform a successful transplant of a human organ—a kidney—in 1954.*

# *Physics*

1901 Wilhelm K. Roentgen *(Germany), for discovery of Roentgen rays*

1902 Hendrik A. Lorentz *and* Pieter Zeeman *(Netherlands), for work on influence of magnetism upon radiation*

1903 A. Henri Becquerel *(France), for work on spontaneous radioactivity, and* Pierre *and* Marie Curie *(France), for study of radiation*

1904 John Strutt (Lord Rayleigh) *(England), for discovery of argon in investigating gas density*

1905 Philipp Lenard *(Germany), for work with cathode rays*

1906 Sir Joseph Thomson *(England), for investigations on passage of electricity through gases*

1907 Albert A. Michelson *(U.S.), for spectroscopic and metrologic investigations*

1908 Gabriel Lippmann *(France), for method of reproducing colors by photography*

1909 Guglielmo Marconi *(Italy), and* Ferdinand Braun *(Germany), for development of wireless*

1910 Johannes D. van der Waals *(Netherlands), for work with the equation of state for gases and liquids*

1911 Wilhelm Wien *(Germany), for his laws governing the radiation of heat*

1912 Gustaf Dalén *(Sweden), for discovery of automatic regulators used in lighting lighthouses and light buoys*

1913 Heike Kamerlingh-Onnes *(Netherlands), for work leading to production of liquid helium*

1914 Max von Laue *(Germany), for discovery of diffraction of Roentgen rays passing through crystals*

1915 Sir William Bragg *and* William L. Bragg *(England), for analysis of crystal structure by X rays*

1916 No award

1917 Charles G. Barkla *(England), for discovery of Roentgen radiation of the elements*

1918 Max Planck *(Germany), discoveries in connection with quantum theory*

1919 Johannes Stark *(Germany), discovery of Doppler effect in Canal rays and decomposition of spectrum lines by electric fields*

1920 Charles E. Guillaume *(Switzerland), for discoveries of anomalies in nickel steel alloys*

1921 Albert Einstein *(Germany), for discovery of the law of the photoelectric effect*

1922 Niels Bohr *(Denmark), for investigation of structure of atoms and radiations emanating from them*

1923 Robert A. Milikan *(U.S.), for work on elementary charge of electricity and photoelectric phenomena*

1924 Karl M. G. Siegbahn *(Sweden), for investigations in X-ray spectroscopy*

1925 James Franck *and* Gustav Hertz *(Germany), for discovery of laws governing impact of electrons upon atoms*

1926 Jean B. Perrin *(France), for work on discontinous structure of matter and discovery of the equilibrium of sedimentation*

1927 Arthur H. Compton *(U.S.), for discovery of Compton phenomenon; and* Charles T. R. Wilson *(England), for method of perceiving paths taken by electrically charged particles*

1928 *In 1929, the 1928 prize was awarded to* Sir Owen Richardson *(England), for work on the phenomenon of thermionics and discovery of the Richardson Law*

1929 Prince Louis Victor de Broglie *(France), for discovery of the wave character of electrons*

1930 Sir Chandrasekhara Raman *(India), for work on diffusion of light and discovery of the Raman effect*

1931 No award

1932 *In 1933, the prize for 1932 was awarded to* Werner Heisenberg *(Germany), for creation of the quantum mechanics*

1933 Erwin Schrödinger *(Austria) and* Paul A. M. Dirac *(England), for discovery of new fertile forms of the atomic theory*

1934 No award

1935 James Chadwick *(England), for discovery of the neutron*

1936 Victor F. Hess *(Austria), for discovery of cosmic radiation; and* Carl D. Anderson *(U.S.), for discovery of the positron*

1937 Clinton J. Davisson *(U.S.) and* George P. Thomson *(England), for discovery of diffraction of electrons by crystals*

1938 Enrico Fermi *(Italy), for identification of new radioactivity elements and discovery of nuclear reactions effected by slow neutrons*

1939 Ernest Orlando Lawrence *(U.S.), for development of the cyclotron*

1943 Otto Stern *(U.S.), for detection of magnetic momentum of protons*

1944 Isidor Isaac Rabi *(U.S.), for work on magnetic movements of atomic particles*

1945 Wolfgang Pauli *(Austria), for work on atomic fissions*

1946 Percy Williams Bridgman *(U.S.), for studies and inventions in high-pressure physics*

1947 Sir Edward Appleton *(England), for discovery of layer which reflects radio short waves in the ionosphere*

1948 Patrick M. S. Blackett *(England), for improvement on Wilson chamber and discoveries in cosmic radiation*

1949 Hideki Yukawa *(Japan), for mathematical prediction, in 1935, of the meson*

1950 Cecil Frank Powell *(England), for method of photographic study of atom nucleus, and for discoveries about mesons*

1951 Sir John Douglas Cockcroft *(England), and* Ernest T. S. Walton *(Ireland), for work in 1932 on transmutation of atomic nuclei*

1952 Edward Mills Purcell *and* Felix Bloch *(U.S.), for work in measurement of magnetic fields in atomic nuclei*

1953 Fritz Zernike *(Netherlands), for development of "phase contrast" microscope*

1954 Max Born *(England), for work in quantum mechanics; and* Walther Bothe *(Germany), for work in cosmic radiation*

1955 Polykarp Kusch *and* Willis E. Lamb, Jr. *(U.S.), for atomic measurements*

1956 William Shockley, Walter H. Brattain, *and* John Bardeen *(U.S.), for developing electronic transistor*

1957 Tsung Dao Lee *and* Chen Ning Yang *(China), for disproving principle of conservation of parity*

1958 Pavel A. Cherenkov, Ilya M. Frank, *and* Igor E. Tamm *(U.S.S.R), for work resulting in development of cosmic-ray counter*

1959 Emilio Segre *and* Owen Chamberlain *(U.S.), for demonstrating the existence of the anti proton*

1960 Donald A. Glaser *(U.S.), for invention of "bubble chamber" to study subatomic particles*

1961 Robert Hofstadter *(U.S.), for determination of shape and size of atomic nucleus; Rudolf Mössbauer (Germany), for method of producing and measuring recoil-free gamma rays*

1962 Lev D. Landau *(U.S.S.R), for his theories about condensed matter*

1963 Eugene Paul Wigner, Maria Goeppert Mayer *(both U.S.), and J. Hans D. Jensen (Germany), for research on structure of atom and its nucleus*

1964 Charles Hard Townes *(U.S.),* Nikolai G. Basov, *and* Aleksandr M. Prochorov (both U.S.S.R), *for developing maser and laser principle of producing high-intensity radiation*

1965 Richard P. Feynman, Julian S. Schwinger *(both U.S.), and* Shinichiro Tomonaga *(Japan), for research in quantum electrodynamics*

1966 Alfred Kastler *(France), for work on energy levels inside atom*

1967 Hans A. Bethe *(U.S.), for work on energy production of stars*

1968 Luis Walter Alvarez *(U.S.), for study of sub-atomic particles*

1969 Murray Gell-Mann *(U.S.), for study of sub-atomic particles*

1970 Hannes Alfvén *(Sweden), for theories in plasma physics; and* Louis Néel *(France), for discoveries in antiferromagnetism and ferrimagnetism*

1971 Dennis Gabor *(England), for invention of holographic method of three-dimensional imagery*

1972 John Bardeen, Leon N. Cooper, *and* John Robert Schrieffer *(all U.S.), for theory of superconductivity, where electrical resistance in certain metals vanishes above absolute zero temperature*

1973 Ivar Giaever *(U.S.),* Leo Esaki *(Japan), and* Brian D. Josephson *(U.K.), for theories that have advanced and expanded the field of miniature electronics*

1974 Antony Hewish *(England), for discovery of pulsars;* Martin Ryle *(England), for using radio-telescopes to probe outer space with highdegree of precision*

1975 James Rainwater *(U.S.) and* Ben Mottelson *and* Aage N. Bohr *(both Denmark), for showing that the atomic nucleus is asymmetrical*

1976 Burton Richter *and* Samuel C. C. Ting *(both U.S.), for discovery of subatomic particles known as J and psi*

1977 Philip W. Anderson *and* John H. Van Vleck *(both U.S.), and* Nevill F. Mott *(U.K.), for work underlying computer memories and electonic devices*

1978 Arno A. Penzias *and* Robert W. Wilson *(both U.S.), for work in cosmic microwave radiation;* Piotr L. Kakpitsa *(U.S.S.R), for basic inventions and discoveries in low-temperature physics*

1979 Steven Weinberg *and* Sheldon L. Glashow *(both U.S.) and* Abdus Salam *(Pakistan), for developing theory that electromagnetism and the "weak" force, which causes radioactive decay in some atomic nuclei, are facets of the same phenomenon*

1980 James W. Cronin *and* Val L. Fitch *(both U.S.), for work concerning the assymetry of subatomic particles*

1981 Nicolaas Bloembergen *and* Arthur L. Schawlow *(both U.S.) and* Kai M. Siegbahn *(Sweden), for developing technologies with lasers and other devices to probe the secrets of complex forms of matter*

1982 Kenneth G. Wilson *(U.S.), for analysis of changes in matter under pressure and temperature*

1983 Subrahmanyam Chandrasekhar *and* William A. Fowler *(both U.S.), for complementary research on processes involved in the evolution of stars*

1984 Carlo Rubbia *(Italy) and* Simon van der Meer *(Netherlands), for their role in discovering three subatomic particles, a step toward developing a single theory to account for all natural forces*

1985 Klaus von Klitzing *(Germany), for developing an exact way of measuring electrical conductivity*

1986 Ernst Ruska, Gerd Binnig *(both Germany) and* Heinrich Rohrer *(Switzerland), for work on microscopes*

1987 K. Alex Müller (Switzerland) *and* J. Georg Bednorz *(Germany), for their discovery of high-temperature superconductors*

1988 Leon M. Ledeman, Melvin Schwartz, Jack Steinberger, *(all U.S.), for research that improved the understanding of elementary particles and forces*

1989 Norman F. Ramsey *(U.S.), for the development during the late 1940's and the 1950's of the cesium atomic clock now commonly used to measure the vibrations of atoms.* Hans G. Demelt *(U.S.) and* Wolfgang Paul *(Germany), for the development of methods to isolate atoms and sub-atomic particles for detailed study*

1990 Jerome Friedman, Kenry Kendall *(both U.S.), and* Richard Taylor *(Canada), for first detecting the existence of quarks and establishing the quark model of matter, which was a milestone in the search for simplicity at the deepest levels of nature in the 1960's*

# *Chemistry*

1901 Jacobus H. van't Hoff *(Netherlands), for laws of chemical dynamics and osmotic pressure in solutions*

1902 Emil Fischer *(Germany), for experiments in sugar and purin groups of substances*

1903 Svante A. Arrhenius *(Sweden), for his electrolytic theory of dissociation*

1904 Sir William Ramsay *(England), for discovery and determination of place of inert gaseous elements in air*

1905 Adolf von Baeyer *(Germany), for work on organic dyes and hydroaromatic combinations*

1906 Henri Moissan *(France), for isolation of fluorine, and introduction of electric furnace*

1907 Eduard Buchner *(Germany), for discovery of cell-less fermintation and investigations in biological chemistry*

1908 Sir Ernest Rutherford *(England), for investigations into disintegration of elements*

1909 Wihelm Ostwald *(Germany), for work on catalysis and investigations into chemical equilibrium and reactions rates*

1910 Otto Wallach *(Germany), for work in the field of alicyclic compounds*

1911 Marie Curie *(France), for discovery of elements radium and polonium*

1912 Victor Grignard *(France), for reagent discovered by him; and* Paul Sabatier *(France), for methods of hydrogenating organic compounds*

1913 Alfred Werner *(Switzerland), for linking up atoms within the molecule*

1914 Theodore W. Richards *(U.S.), for determining atomic weight of many chemical elements*

1915 Richard Willstätter *(Germany), for research into coloring matter of plants, especially chlorophyll*

1916 No award

1917 No award

1918 Fritz Harber *(Germany), for synthetic production of ammonia*

1919 No award

1920 Walther Nernst *(Germany), for work in thermochemistry*

1921 Frederick Soddy *(England), for investigations into origin and nature of isotopes*

1922 Francis W. Aston *(England), for discovery of isotopes in nonradioactive elements and for discovery of the whole number rule*

1923 Fritz Pregl *(Austria), for method of microanalysis of organic substances discovered by him*

1924 No award

1925 *In 1926, the 1925 prize was awarded to* Richard Zsigmondy *(Germany), for work on the heterogeneous nature of colloid solutions*

1926 Theodor Svedberg *(Sweden), for work on disperse systems*

1927 *In 1928, the 1927 prize was awarded to* Heinrich Wieland *(Germany), for investigations of bile acids and kindred substances*

1928 Adolf Windaus *(Germany), for investigations on constitution of the sterols and their connection with vitamins*

**Chemistry, continued**

1929 Sir Arthur Harden *(England), and* Hans K. A. S. von Euler-Chelpin *(Sweden), for research of fermentation of sugars*

1930 Hans Fischer *(Germany), for work on coloring matter of blood and leaves and for his synthesis of hemin*

1931 Karl Bosch *and* Friedrich Bergius *(Germany), for invention and development of chemical high-pressure methods*

1932 Irving Langmuir *(U.S.), for work in realm of surface chemistry*

1933 No award

1934 Harold C. Urey *(U.S.), for discovery of heavy hydrogen*

1935 Frédéric *and* Irène Joliot-Curie *(France), for synthesis of new radioactive elements*

1936 Peter J. W. Debye *(Netherlands), for investigations on dipole moments and diffraction of X-rays and electrons in gases*

1937 Walter N. Haworth *(England), for research on carbohydrates and Vitamin C; and* Paul Karrer *(Switzerland), for work on carotenoids, flavins, and Vitamins A and B*

1938 Richard Kuhn *(Germany), for carotinoid study and vitamin research (declined)*

1939 Adolf Butenandt *(Germany), for work on sexual hormones (declined); and* Leopold Ruzicka *(Switzerland), for work with polymethylenes*

1943 Georg Hevesy De Heves *(Hungary), for work on use of isotopes as indicators*

1944 Otto Hahn *(Germany), for work on atomic fission*

1945 Artturi Illmari Virtanen *(Finland), for research in the field of conservation of fodder*

1946 James B. Summer *(U.S.), for crystallizing enzymes;* John H. Northrop *and* Wendell M. Stanley *(U.S.), for preparing enzymes and virus proteins in pure form*

1947 Sir Robert Robinson *(England), for research in plant substances*

1948 Arne Tiselius *(Sweden), for biochemical discoveries and isolation of mouse paralysis virus*

1949 William Francis Giauque *(U.S.), for research in thermodynamics, especially effects of low temperature*

1950 Otto Diels *and* Kurt Alder *(Germany), for discovery of diene synthesis enabling scientists to study structure of organic matter*

1951 Glenn T. Seaborg *and* Edwin H. McMillan *(U.S.), for discovery of plutonium*

1952 Archer John Porter Martin *and* Richard Laurence Millington Synge *(England), for development of partition chromatography*

1953 Hermann Staudinger *(Germany), for research in giant molecules*

1954 Linus C. Pauling *(U.S.), for study of forces holding together protein and other molecules*

1955 Vincent du Vigneaud *(U.S.), for work on pituitary hormones*

1956 Sir Cyril Hinshelwood *(England), and* Nikolai N. Semenov *(U.S.S.R), for parallel research on chemical reaction kinetics*

1957 Sir Alexander Todd *(England), for research with chemical compounds that are factors in heredity*

1958 Frederick Sanger *(England), for determining molecular structure of insulin*

1959 Jaroslav Heyrovsky *(Czechoslovakia), for development of polarography, an electrochemical method of analysis*

1960 Willard F. Libby *(U.S.), for "atomic time clock" to measure age of objects by measuring their radioactivity*

1961 Melvin Calvin *(U.S.), for establishing-chemical steps during photosynthesis*

1962 Max F. Perutz *and* John C. Kendrew *(England), for mapping protein molecules with X-rays*

1963 Carl Ziegler *(Germany), and* Giulio Natta *(Italy), for work in uniting simple hydrocarbons into large molecule substances*

1964 Dorothy Mary Crowfoot Hodgkin *(England), for determining structure of compounds needed in combating pernicious anemia*

1965 Robert B. Woodward *(U.S.), for work in synthesizing complicated organic compounds*

1966 Robert Sanderson Mulliken *(U.S.), for research on bond holding atoms together in molecule*

1967 Manfred Eigen *(Germany),* Ronald G. W. Norrish, *and* George Porter *(both England), for work in high-speed chemical reactions*

1968 Lars Onsager *(U.S.), for development of system of equations in thermodynamics*

1969 Derek H. R. Barton *(England), and* Odd Hassel *(Norway), for study of organic molecules*

1970 Luis F. Leloir *(Argentina), for discovery of sugar nucleotides and their role in biosynthesis of carbohydrates*

1971 Gerhard Herzberg *(Canada), for contributions to knowledge of electronic structure and geometry of molecules, particularly free radicals*

1972 Christian Boehmer Anfinsen, Stanford Moore, *and* William Howard Stein *(all U.S.), for pioneering studies in enzymes*

1973 Ernst Otto Fischer *(W. Germany), and* Geoffrey Wilkinson *(U.K.), for work that could solve problem of automobile exhaust pollution*

1974 Paul J. Flory *(U.S.), for developing analytic methods to study properties and molecular structure of long-chain molecules*

1975 John W. Cornforth *(Australia) and* Vladimir Prelog *(Switzerland), for research on structure of biological molecules such as antibiotics and cholesterol*

1976 William N. Lipscomb, Jr. *(U.S.), for work on the structure and bonding mechanisms of boranes*

1977 Ilya Prigogine *(Belgium), for contributions to nonequilibrium thermodynamics, particularly the theory of dissipative structures*

1978 Peter Mitchell *(U.K.), for contributions to the understanding of biological energy transfer*

1979 Herbert C. Brown *(U.S.), and* Georg Wittig *(W. Germany), for developing a group of substances that facilitate very difficult chemical reactions*

1980 Paul Berg *and* Walter Gilbert *(both U.S.), and* Frederick Sanger *(England), for developing methods to map function of DNA, the substance that controls the activity of the cell*

1981 Roald Hoffmann *(U.S.), and* Kenichi Fukui *(Japan), for applying quantum-mechanics theories to predict the course of chemical reactions*

1982 Aaron Klug *(U.K.), for research in the detailed structures of viruses and components of life*

1983 Henry Taube *(U.S.), for research on how electrons transfer between molecules in chemical reactions*

1984 R. Bruce Merrifield *(U.S.), for research that revolutionized the study of proteins*

1985 Herbert A. Hauptman *and* Jerome Karle *(both U.S.), for their outstanding achievements in the development of direct methods for the determination of crystal structures*

1986 Dudley R. Herschback, Yuan T. Lee *(both U.S.), and* John C. Polanyi *(Canada), for their work on "reaction dynamics"*

1987 Donald J. Cram *and* Charles J. Pedersen *(both U.S.), and* Jean-Marie Lehn *(France), for wideranging research that has included the creation of artificial molecules that can mimic vital chemical reactions of the processes of life*

1988 Dr. Hohann Deisenhofer, Dr. Robert Huber *and* Dr. Harmut Michel *(all W. Germany), for unraveling the structure of proteins that play a crucial role in photosynthesis*

1989 Thomas R. Cech *and* Sidney Altman *(both U.S.), for discovering independently that the substance RNA was not just a passive carrier of genetic information, but could actively aid chemical reaction in cells*

1990 Elias James Corey *(U.S.), for pioneering "retrosynthetic analysis," an approach of breaking down compounds, bond by bond, into smaller and smaller components.*

# Key Word Index

133

# Bibliography

## Books

Anderson, Erica. *The World of Albert Schweitzer*. New York: Harper & Row Publishers, 1955.

Buck, Pearl S. *My Several Worlds*. New York: The John Day Co., 1954

Clark, Ronald W. *The Life and Times of Einstein*. New York: Harry N. Abrams, Inc., 1984.

Craig, Mary. *Lech Walesa and His Poland*. New York: Continuum Publishing Co., 1986.

Dalai Lama, *My Land and My People*. New York: McGraw-Hill Book Company, Inc., 1962.

Dukas, Helen, and Banesh Hoffman eds. *Albert Einstein: The Human Side*. Princeton: Princeton University Press, 1979.

Friedman, Milton. *Capitalism and Freedom*. Chicago: University of Chicago Press (Phoenix Books), 1962.

Garciá Gabriel Márquez. *One Hundred Years of Solitude*. New York: Avon Books, 1970.

Infeld, Leopold. *Albert Einstein: His Work and Its Influence On Our World*. New York: Charles Scribner's Sons, 1950.

McConnell, Campbell R. *Economics*. Eighth edition. New York: McGraw-Hill Book Co., 1981

McKown, Robin. *She Lived for Science: Irène Joliot-Curie*. New York: Julian Messner, Inc., 1961.

Meyer, Edith Patterson. *Dynamite and Peace*. Boston: Little, Brown and Co., 1958

Meyer, Edith Patterson. *In Search of Peace*. Nashville: Abingdon, 1978.

Miller, William Robert. *Martin Luther King, Jr.: His Life, Martyrdom, and Meaning for the World*. New York: Weybright and Talley, 1968.

Nathan, Otto, and Heinz Norden, eds. *Einstein on Peace*. New York: Avenel Books 1981.

Russell, Bertrand. *The Autobiography of Bertrand Russell*. New York: Simon and Schuster, 1969.

Russell, Bertrand. *Human Society in Ethics and Politics*. New American Library (A Mentor Book), 1962.

Russell, Bertrand. *The Impact of Science on society.* New York: Simon and Schuster, 1953.

Sakharov, Andrei D. *My Country and the World.* New York: Alfred A. Knopf, 1975

Samuelson, Paul. *Economics From the Heart.* New York: Harcourt Brace Javanovich, Publishers, 1983.

Silk, Leonard. *Economics in Plain English.* New York: Simon and Schuster, 1978.

Silk, Leonard. *Economists.* New York: Basic Books Inc., 1974.

Spencer, Cornelia. *The Exile's Daughter: A Biography of Pearl S. Buck.* New York: Coward-McCann, Inc., 1944.

Spink, Kathryn. *The Miracle of Love: Mother Teresa of Calcutta, Her Missionaries of Charity, and Co-Workers.* San Francisco, California: Harper and Row Publishers, 1981.

Stern, Ellen Norman. *Elie Wiesel: Witness For Life.* New York: KTAV Publishing House, Inc., 1982

Tutu, Desmond. *Hope and Suffering.* Michigan: William B. Eerdmans Publishing Co., 1984.

Walesa, Lech. *Lech Walesa: A Way of Hope.* New York: Henry Holt and Co., 1987

## Reference Texts

*Collier's Encyclopedia,* 1985 Ed.,
  S.v. "Martin Luther King, Jr."
  S.v. "Mother Teresa."
  S.v. "Desmont Tutu."
  S.v. "Andrei Sakharov."
  S.v. "Albert Schweitzer."
  S.v. "Elie Wiesel."

*Current Biography Yearbook.* New York: H.W. Wilson, vols. 1940, 1946, 1973, 1981, 1982, 1987, 1989.

Frenz, Hurst ed. *Nobel Lectures-Literature.* New York: Elsevier Publishing Co., 1969.

Schlessinger, Bernard S., and Jene H. Schlessinger, eds. *The Who's Who of Nobel Prize Winners.* Phoenix, AZ: Oryx Press, 1986.

Sicherman, Barbara, and Carol Green, eds. *Notable American Women: The Modern Period.* Cambridge, Mass.: The Belknap Press of Harvard University Press, 1980.

## Magazines

Ahmed, Hamed Abu. "A Nobelist's Inspiration." *World Press Review*, January, 1989 p. 61.

"A Bow to Tibet." *Time*, 16 October 1989, p. 44.

"China's Nobel Rebuke." *Newsweek*, 16 October 1989, p. 54.

Dickey, Christopher. "A Baedeker to Egypt's Soul. (Mahfouz's masterpiece is published in English)." *Newsweek*, 5 March 1990, p. 48.

Forbes, Malcolm S. "Fact and Comment: You Don't Have to Be a Buddhist to Dig The Dalai Lama." *Forbes*, 4 September 1989, pp. 19-20.

Steif, William. "Naguib Mahfouz: Fifteen minutes with Egypt's Nobel laureate." *The Progressive*, February 1989, pp. 38-39.

Watson, Russell, Scott Sullivan, Thomas M. DeFrank, and Fred Coleman. "Freedom's Turn." *Newsweek*, 28 August 1989, pp. 16-21.

## Newspapers

Richards, Carol R. "The Holocaust: Once a year, at least, we must feel the pain." *USA Today*, 28 April 1987, p. 11A.

Wilford, John Noble. "2 Americans Win Nobel Medicine Prize." *The New York Times*, 15 October 1985, p. A1.